JUST LAUGH ABOUT IT

Improve your health
Reduce your stress and tensions

Sid Baron

2008

SID BARON

JUST LAUGH ABOUT IT

Published by:
Exxel Publishing Co.
323 Telegraph Rd.
Bellingham, WA 98226
Tel.: 360-671-2275

Ordering information

Visit www.sidbaron.com for easy on-line ordering.
Contact author via e-mail: sietze@msn.com

Mail your order to:
Exxel Publishing Co.
323 Telegraph Rd.
Bellingham, WA 98226

Enclose $14.95 plus $2.95 postage (Canada $4.95) for each copy ordered.
Inquire about quantity discounts.

Ordering by telephone or fax:
Telephone: 360-671-2275
Fax: 360-671-7616

ISBN 978-0-9703469-0-2

Library of Congress Control Number: 2007935062

Table of Contents

Dedication

This book is dedicated to all former as well as current associates whom I've had the pleasure of working with thru-out my varied business career. Some of them may never have been aware of the humorous and "naughty" side of my personality. Some would likely not believe that it is still there. After laughing their way through this book they may become suspicious that they could still become a victim at any time.

Introduction

If you've paged through this book and read either of my two previous books, you may wonder why I would write a book seemingly for the sole purpose of making the reader laugh. The answer is a little complicated. My best seller *The Way it Was* is a compilation of events that I experienced and witnessed primarily during WW II while living in German occupied Holland. *Just Laugh about it* is a compilation of true events that occurred during my career in America.

As you read this book you will soon learn that I subjected myself to enormous physical and emotional stresses during my multi-faceted career. It wasn't until later that I learned that my frequent bouts of illnesses were related to stress. And a few years later I was officially diagnosed with Multiple Sclerosis. I learned that MS is an incurable, progressive neurological disease. I was scared and decided to learn everything I possibly could about the potential devastating effects of Multiple Sclerosis. You may not suffer from MS, but whatever your position or work activities in life, you experience stress. It is unavoidable. It is not only the number one enemy of MS, it is the number one impediment to living a healthy, happy life.

I read *The Anatomy of an Illness* by Norman Cousins. He suffered from Ankylosing Spondylitis, a life-threatening disease of the joints and connective tissue that left him in excruciating pain with few options for treatment.

After his medical experts had declared that he was incurable and would not have long to live, he discontinued all his medication, including painkillers, and turned to humor and Vitamin C. One of the things Cousins documented was that a 10-minute belly laugh could give him two hours of painless sleep. He says: "What you begin to appreciate is the profound effect that positive emotions can have on your entire physical and emotional being." To the amazement of his medical experts, Mr. Cousins gradually improved and became completely well again. Norman Cousins writes: "Laughter, hope, faith, love, will to live, cheerfulness, humor, creativity, playfulness, confidence, great expectations—all these, have therapeutic value."

"Laughter reduces pain, increases job performance, connects people emotionally, and improves the flow of oxygen to the heart and brain." (**Norman Cousins**)

Studies have shown the following physiological effects of laughter in the immune system alone: increase in the number and activity of T cells and natural killer cells, which attack viruses, foreign cells and cancer cells; increase in gamma interferon, a blood chemical that transmits messages in the nervous system and stimulates the immune system; an antibody that fights, among others, upper respiratory tract infections.

Mirthful laughter has also been shown to exercise the cardiovascular system by raising and lowering the heart rate and blood pressure; improve coordination of brain functions, thereby enhancing alertness and memory; lift depression; reduce stress; bring pain relief; aid ventilation and clear mucus in the respiratory system; increase blood oxygen by bringing in fresh air; and strengthen internal muscles by tightening and releasing them. One doctor says that 20 seconds of guffawing gives the heart the same workout as three minutes of hard rowing.

Whatever your field of activity or responsibility, you experience stress. It is unavoidable. But if you experience relentless and unabated stress it will invariably lead to physical or mental-emotional break-down. You must take action and break the relentless nature of your stress. Humor and laughter will do that. Those who exercise their humor muscles will benefit from reduced stress, greater empathy, and a better ability to relate to your loved ones, coworkers, or subordinates.

Perhaps you are one of a small percentage of people who have difficulty laughing. Life is too serious, too sacred. You may believe that every joke and prank is targeted at a helpless victim. It's not funny—it's cruel. There's plenty of cruelty in life. And none is to be laughed about. As you painfully page through one cruel prank after another, please remember that the "poor victims" were and still are some of my best friends; that together, so many years later, we still laugh about the hilarious events of when the friend became another "poor victim."

Research shows that a small percentage of people truly have a "joyless life." Over time it affects their well being in every area of life. That brings up the question: "can a sense of humor be developed?" Experts say, "yes" but only to a degree. Those who by nature live their life on the heavy side find it difficult to move to the lighter side, even for just a little while.

A plethora of studies have reached the conclusion that humor and laughter can really improve your physical, emotional, and mental health and add years to your life.

Understanding that will help you understand that the true stories you are about to read are not merely a compilation of whimsical events as much as they are essential ingredients that helped me navigate through enormous stresses of life and helped me, I'm convinced, survive MS.

I've had MS for nearly 40 years. I've experienced nearly every devastating symptom of the disease. Yet, were you and I to meet today you would not know that I have MS. Still, not a day goes by that I do not know that I have MS. This book will give you little "snapshots" of life's struggles and stresses. There is no doubt in my mind that my lighthearted sense of humor was, and is, a very important component of surviving MS.

It is my sincere hope that you will not only find this book entertaining reading but that it will enhance your sense of well-being. That's the reason I wrote "Just Laugh about it".

Sid Baron

June 1948

It was an impressive sight.

I stood on the deck of the S.S. Veendam and watched as we cruised past the Statue of Liberty, that world famous symbol of freedom, of possibility, of a bright future. Above the busy harbor, seagulls wheeled, squealing out a message of welcome. A breeze smelling of land and hope ruffled my hair.

This was America! The land of unlimited opportunity I had read about several months before when I still lived in Opende in The Netherlands. This was the America that had sent its soldiers and its airplanes to help liberate Holland from five years of occupation by Hitler's Germany.

It was early in June 1948 when our ship moored in Hoboken, New Jersey, two weeks past my eighteenth birthday. Among the many immigrants who had arrived with me were my parents, my sisters Betty, Greta and Mary, and my brother Henry.

We all felt the excitement of being in the land of unlimited opportunity. Alongside the thrill, though, I felt fear. I was in a foreign land facing a completely unknown future.

I was born in The Netherlands on May 13, 1930. I lived there the first 18 years of my life, including the unforgettable 5-year occupation by Nazi Germany. Many events of that period are written in my previous book *The Way it Was*. Comments from many readers

1

who lived in an occupied country during that time made me realize how experiencing similar events and all sharing the same fears and anxieties connected us. *The Way it Was* made the readers reflect on the experiences of their lives and re-visit their younger years. It's filled not just with the drama of my experiences with the Nazis—but the humor that helped me and my family cope. If you haven't read it, I hope this book piques your curiosity enough to get a copy.

My parents had been farmers back in the Old Country. I knew when I arrived in America I would have to help them get started farming again in a strange land. Deep inside me, though, I yearned for new adventures that had nothing to do with tilling the earth or slopping hogs.

I got my wish, but in ways I could never have imagined.

My first adventure was a young woman. Her name was Margaret Tjoelker. I was to spend the rest of my life with her, but I wasn't thinking about the rest of my life right then!

I met her in Everson, Washington, all the way across the country.

My mother had two cousins in nearby Lynden. They had sponsored our move. They had agreed to be financially responsible for my family for five years. How the immigration laws have changed since then.

We'd taken a train from New York. I remember well stopping in Chicago and seeing a stretch limousine for the very first time. What big automobiles they have in this country, I thought.

And what a huge country!

Five days after leaving the East Coast the train stopped in the small city in the Northwest corner of the United States that was Bellingham. There I was, without money, without a job, with virtually no knowledge of the language of this country I had read so much about while still living in Holland.

Lynden, WA, where I live now, is a small town 15 miles north of Bellingham with a modest population of about 9,000. It lies on the Nooksack River Valley, not far from Bellingham Bay. Lynden is near the Canadian border. It's an easy drive from here to British Columbia. Lynden is a very religious town. At one time it held a world record for the most churches per square miles. On Sunday most of the stores in Lynden shut down so that people can go to church.

Throughout the first half of the twentieth century, Lynden was a favorite destination for immigrants from Holland settling in the U.S. The Dutch language is still spoken by some of the town's residents and Dutch food is sold in the grocery stores and bakeries. Front Street, in the middle of town, was designed with a Dutch theme and even has its own authentic Dutch windmill. Each year a Dutch festival is held. There's a parade and wooden shoe dances. I feel right at home here.

Margaret and I were married on December 14, 1948. We were both 19 years old. Margaret worked as a teller in a bank. I didn't have a job.

There are men who are happy to sit around and let their wives work, but I felt as worthless as an udder on a steer. Using twenty-five cents of Margaret's paycheck I purchased a copy of a magazine entitled *Salesmen's Opportunity.* Soon I was selling floor-waxers door to door.

I didn't sell many waxers at first, but I learned.

Numerous early rejections taught me the art of persuasion. I learned how to be a successful salesman. The secret is to know your message and deliver it well.

Still, I didn't make enough money with the floor-waxers, so in the spring my father-in-law arranged for a loan and helped me purchase a dozen milk cows. I was back on a small farm, alas. I had no interest in making farming my lifetime career but I did have to make a living. Twice a day I milked my cows. In between I practiced my door-to-door selling skills. I had no passion for either squirting milk into pails or extolling the merits of floor waxers.

What I loved was electronics.

I longed for a business of my own that would let me exercise my passion for circuits, wires and electricity.

Only a short time after our marriage Margaret became pregnant. She quit her banking job a few months later. Soon we'd be first-time parents. Jimmy was born and we were now a family of three. In those days, women didn't have babies and then go back to their jobs. They stayed at home and took care of the kids.

I knew I now had the duty of being sole provider for my family.

A voice within me said: "If you have no passion for the way you're making a living now, if you have loftier dreams and ambitions, you need to take action that will push you in the right direction."

I ordered an electronics home study course from DeVry Technical Institute. I started working with resistors, vacuum tubes and a soldering iron, between milking cows, other farm work and door-to-door selling. The need to make a living prevented me from becoming a full time student. But within two years I had opened a small electronics shop in the small town of Lynden, Washington. I began repairing radios, TV's, and other electronic equipment.

Pressures mounted. I was juggling a lot of balls and red-hot soldering irons.

Still, I was just getting started.

Time passed, bringing welcome changes. Soon a storefront was added with electronics inventory, a service department and my first employee. I stopped selling waxers, so I could make service calls in customer homes. The cows, though, still waited for me to milk and feed them. Our family burgeoned to four children, all boys. Margaret was busier now than when she had worked in the bank. Providing for a growing family was a strong motivator even as pressures mounted. But I was young, with boundless energy and ambition. I was building a future in the land of unlimited opportunities. I was enjoying it!

And I was just getting started.

During the Second World War, I had been intrigued by something that occurred to me while I was standing outside looking at the sky. All those bombers and fighter planes flying across Holland on their way to Germany had to communicate with each other as well as with ground control. But how? Well, radio, of course.

Immediately after the war I became fascinated with amateur radio. By the time I had healthy kids and cows, and a healthy electronics business, I had already earned my FCC amateur radio license. I began dreaming of building a commercial broadcast station.

Starting a commercial radio station in the small town of Lynden, Washington, was a crazy idea, some people said. But I persevered. On November 9, 1960, KLYN-FM began broadcasting at 106.5 MHz.

Although I'd learned to sell door-to-door, I didn't particularly like selling radio advertising. I did, however, love every other aspect of the broadcasting business. I particularly enjoyed programming my station. Our schedule included news, sports, editorials, talk shows and call-in programs.

The broadcasting business opened the door to other opportunities. In addition to opening the Lynden Travel Agency my company began supplying background music to stores and restaurants. Success with that led to manufacturing on-premise recorded music systems. I began to employ sales representatives in various parts of the country and established Motivating Sound, Inc.

The number of balls I was now attempting to juggle became, well, simply ridiculous. Fortunately, I was no longer juggling udders.

Still, I needed a diversion, something to take my mind off business. I decided to learn to fly an airplane and become a pilot. With a growing family, Margaret was not excited about the idea of any risk involved, but had to agree that flying was useful. I used my airplane extensively for business purposes. When the wheels lifted from the runway and the airplane broke the surly bonds of earth, I could, even for a short while, leave the ever-mounting cares and responsibilities behind.

Meanwhile, on the ground, I learned more and more about the value of humor to relieve stress. That's what this book is about.

Despite the pleasures of pranks and much lighthearted laughter, the relentless, unabated stress of my complex business juggling act ultimately took a toll. In 1970 I developed multiple sclerosis.

This diagnosis jolted me to a new and greater awareness. I needed to change my lifestyle to include more rest and relaxation, more fun and laughter. I realized how much responsibility I truly had. By this time there were employees whose families depended on the continuation of my businesses for their economic well-being.

I needed to change my life. I needed to become less the hard working do-er, and more a relaxed delegator.

Was this the end of my propensity for spawning new businesses? No.

The change was simply a new beginning.

I entered the field of real estate development. Soon my company's holdings expanded into hotels, apartments, a retirement community and other real estate ownership. With a younger, intelligent, and ambitious partner we founded a small, general construction-contracting business. Thus Exxel Pacific Construction was born. All of this has now grown into activities in various parts of the United States. To reach those far-flung areas we now have a jet aircraft and a helicopter. I also own a Cessna, which I still fly.

❋ ❋ ❋

I should tell you a few things about my family. Jim was the first born of our sons. Margaret and I were both 20 at the time of his birth.

He's a little taller than his dad and probably 20 pounds heavier. He took over Baron Telecommunications during the late 1980s and later sold it. He then became manager of the Northwest Washington Fair in Lynden, a position he currently holds. He and his wife Laurie have two children and three grandchildren. He is a very likeable man who enjoys fishing and counseling people with addiction problems.

Gerald was our second-born son. His wife is named Lynn and together they have three children and are currently expecting their fifth grandchild. Gerald is an excellent writer; one of his books is published by Prentice Hall. He earned a master's degree in communications as well as an honorary Ph.D. He started his own business in Bellingham and is the CEO of Pier Systems, a Web-based business he founded that sells emergency communication systems to many Fortune 500 companies across the U.S. He is frequently asked to speak to business executives in different cities. He's about an inch or so taller than I am and weighs about 175 lbs.

Ron is son number three. He and his wife Natalie live in Yakima, WA. They have four children and are expecting their first grandchild. Like his dad, Ron is a born entrepreneur. He is also an excellent writer and has a fun-loving personality. Natalie is a registered nurse working in a Yakima hospital. Like our other children, both are excellent parents and have a close-knit family. Ron keeps coming up with new business ideas and, while currently in the process of implementing a new business venture, is in the process of selling his Web-based business. He stands a little over six feet tall and, like his dad, had a thick mane of curly hair that started thinning a number of years ago. My thick curly hair largely disappeared.

Alan is our fourth and youngest son. He is much like his mother in a number of ways. He's the general manager of two family-owned hotels in Bellingham. Alan and his wife Debbie have three children and are expecting two more grandchildren, in addition to little Emma.

Alan has experienced much illness in his life. He was a victim of early-onset diabetes. In addition, he was diagnosed with liver disease nearly 20 years ago and given 12 years to live. He grew steadily worse but was blessed with a liver transplant a few years ago and is now doing well. He has a very strong faith that has carried him and his family through many dark valleys. He is involved in many church activities and also loves to golf.

After four sons, Margaret and I were both surprised when Kaye-Lynn was born, early in 1961. Her name came from my radio station, KLYN-FM, which the announcers pronounce as "K-Lyn." During her high school years she even served as a disc jockey for us. She grew up to be a very attractive and outgoing young lady of about 5'10" or so. She has always loved to laugh heartily and is usually the belle of any party she attends. She married at 18 or 19, but unfortunately her husband was physically abusive and the marriage lasted less than a year. After a couple of jobs in sales, she decided to go school. She earned her Ph.D. in clinical psychology and, after working for the Federal prison system, opened her own practice in Colorado Springs. She never married again and is very successful in her practice.

About two years after Kaye-Lynn was born, our second daughter, sixth and last child, Julie-Ann was born. Julie was the youngest. All her older siblings adored her. When each morning they left for school, Julie stood on a chair by the door to kiss them all "good bye." Her kind loving and caring nature never left her. Not even after she was nearly killed by a drunk driver. She was blessed with a son and a daughter and is an Administrative Assistant at a local Retirement Center.

※ ※ ※

After a long, fruitful life of accomplishment, I've learned much.

What I'd like to suggest here, though, is that if you have ambitious plans for starting a complicated new business, you need to read about keeping your stress level in check.

It is my hope and dearest wish that this book might provide many laughs on its own. But I also hope you discover many ideas here on how you can nurture and develop your own sense of humor.

A sense of humor is a wonderful way to maintain sanity in any busy, pressure-filled life.

The Shock

"We service everything we sell!"

That was our advertising motto at the first electronics store I owned and operated in Lynden, Washington. This was in the 1950s, and I discovered the same secret that made Sam Walton of Wal-Mart a success. Make your customer happy!

What made customers happiest was the fact that our service department worked on pretty much anything and everything that they brought in, a fact that led to one of my most memorable practical jokes.

No, at *Baron's TV and Radio* we didn't limit our electronics service department to only the brands that we sold in our store; we would service anything with a plug or a battery.

Remember those old phonographs, the ones with the record changers? The ones that played discs made of vinyl, the stuff we used long before the digital age? Now if those phonograph changers worked properly, you could load several records on the spindle. The unit would drop a disc onto the turntable, swing the needle over it, drop it into a groove, play the record, swing the arm back, and drop the next record.

Or at least it would perform this Rube Goldberg-like dance when the intricate mechanical mechanism worked properly!

Our customers did not differentiate between the electronic and mechanical aspects of their stereo systems. We got a lot of record changer problems at our service shop. People expected us to repair problems that caused the changer to drop several records at the same time or fail to drop the next record at all.

Now, I was certainly no genius at things mechanical. Jake, our chief electronic technician, was slightly better, but even Jake would prefer passing the buck on mechanical systems that needed repair.

One year we hired a smart young Western Washington University student. Richard could take apart the entire engine of his old Volkswagen convertible. Even if these parts got scattered helter-skelter all over a cluttered garage, Richard would get that VW engine back together and purring again. Of course, a record changer mechanism was nothing like an automobile engine. There were no pistons, carburetor or spark plugs. But since Richard was very analytical, he was confident that if he were able to observe one going through its cycle, he could find and fix the problem.

One day, a malfunctioning stereo came in. Problem? Faulty record changer.

Jake and I were amused at how cocky and confident Richard was about his gift for mechanics. Things had been busy lately. Maybe it was time for a laugh!

Whether that little devil had been on Jake's shoulder or mine, I don't remember. Our plan, though, was shockingly fiendish.

We attached the changer to a bracket mounted high on the workbench. It was a bracket specially designed to allow technicians to observe a record-changing mechanism and cause it to simulate a normal cycle in slow motion.

For some time we had had an old Model T Ford ignition coil at the shop. The Model T had been a popular car in the 1920s, but not many remained in the 1950s. This ignition coil had no practical uses—except for practical jokes. We knew that Richard was scheduled to work on the record changer the following afternoon when he came in to work after his college classes.

Jake and I prepared this ignition coil to deliver an enormous spark at the push of a small button. In the evening I ran a completely hidden wire from the coil to the bracket that held the changer mechanism. Even the German Gestapo search experts back in Holland during World War II wouldn't have discovered this set-up.

There was only one little problem.

Neither Jake nor I were excited about being the guinea pig who tested this jape to make sure it would work! We would just have to wait and see.

It was about two in the afternoon when Richard arrived at the shop. I told him that neither Jake nor I had been able to find what was wrong with this blasted record changer! Gosh, Richard! We're banking on your genius to fix it!

Oh, yes, indeed, this was the kind of challenge Richard loved. He proceeded to study the workings of the mechanism intently.

Jake was busy soldering a resistor into the circuitry of a television chassis turned sideways. I had just completed a sale. When Jake heard the customer leave, he took his place at the executioner's switch.

I stood behind Richard, making sure there was plenty of distance between us. I asked him if he had come up with any ideas about the nature of the problem.

"Well, Sid," intoned Richard with great gravity. "I think this little lever is bind. . . . .OUCH!"

Richard jumped back.

"YIKES!! What the #@*#@ was that?"

He stared at his hand, looking for a scorch mark where the "lightning" had struck him.

Jake pretended to be concentrating on his TV repair work. Succeeding in stifling my own laughter, I asked, "What happened, Rich?"

"Oh, man, I got one heck of a shock. Did you see that spark? It was nearly two inches."

"Shock?" I said, examining the area. "Rich, you could hardly have gotten a shock. Look, the mechanism isn't even plugged in. It's not connected to anything. And you sure didn't get hit by lightning. There's not a cloud in the sky."

Richard ascertained that the unit was not connected to a power source and proceeded to analyze the problem. All went well for about ten minutes.

Fortunately, there were no customers in earshot when Rich got struck by lightning for the second time.

He employed all the power of his vocal cords when he yelled, "YIKES. . . . HOLY MOLY . . . IT GOT ME AGAIN!" He yelled with all the power in his vocal cords. "What in the world is going on?"

Richard stood there with a totally perplexed look on his face, shaking his "bitten" hand.

Suppressing laughter again I said, "Richard, how can it be? Are you sure the spark didn't come out of *you* and hit the changer?"

"I don't know *what* to think," Richard said. "All I know is that I had just figured out that the problem was with the spindle when I got zapped again."

"That's good, Rich. You're almost done. I'm sure you won't get zapped again." "Hey, man, I'm not taking a chance on that."

With that pronouncement, he headed out of the front door into the street. Ten minutes later he came back with a pair of gloves the size of frying pans.

Now I could safely laugh. "Boy, nothing is going to get through those big gloves, Rich," I said.

He didn't respond. He clumsily turned his attention to the machine again. Just as he was forcing the mechanism through a record-changing cycle, Jake pushed the button again.

Instantly Richard howled with distress.

"Right through my gloves," he said. "I've got rubber soles on my shoes. I know I'm not grounded. The changer isn't connected to anything. What in the world is going on here?"

Richard was a curious, intelligent, resourceful guy. He stood there, staring at the thing that kept biting him. Then, removing his gloves, he disappeared into the back of the building. Within minutes he returned, carrying an old rubber tire. He placed the tire on the floor, put on his heavy gloves, stood on top of the tire and proceeded to put the machine through one more record-changing cycle. Jake remained bent over his TV chassis, concentrating on his work, when he inconspicuously pushed the button again.

I cannot print any of the words that escaped from Richard's mouth.

He pulled of his gloves and gave that rubber tire a mighty kick. He practically flew out of the store toward his car and headed for home.

It had been the most shocking day in Richard's life.

Cousin Lukey

I was under a lot of pressure that day. Not even the prospect of a plane trip was doing much for me.

The small four-place Piper Tripacer airplane hurdled down runway 16 at Bellingham International Airport. I watched the airspeed indicator and when it approached 65 miles per hour I gently pulled back on the control yoke. The wheels lifted from the runway and the airplane again seemed to break the law of gravity. I made a shallow left climbing turn and leveled out on a compass heading that pointed me in the direction of Portland, Oregon.

One of our background music units, complete with a supply of sample tapes, rested on the floor of the plane's small cargo area.

I was on the way to see a potential customer for our four channel background music machines. Fortunately the weather was clear and my earlier aviation weather briefing indicated that it was expected to remain clear for at least the next 24 hours.

Several hours later on my flight back to Bellingham I was elated. The first order for a small quantity of our background music machines was in my coat pocket. At the same time I felt the pressures I'd felt that morning mounting. My demonstration unit was a prototype. Now I needed to seriously think and plan setting up an assembly line in the rear of our radio TV service department to begin manufacturing a small quantity of our background music tape players. That included ordering every part and component that went into our unit in quantity. We need to hire and train electronics assembly personnel, and set quality control and testing procedures as well as a complete cost control accounting system.

My head was spinning

Fortunately my airplane was not.

It droned along in smooth air until the wheels and tires were required to instantly start spinning furiously as they touched the runway.

After dinner that evening our neighbors Bob and his wife came over for a friendly visit.

We had already moved off the farm and lived at 211 Front Street in Lynden, WA. At that time the last two hours of the broadcast day for KLYN-FM radio station were automated.

At 10 o'clock each evening I had to make the final sign-off announcement and turn off the transmitter and other studio equipment.

I invited Bob along to the radio station and we both walked the four blocks. I told him about the pressures I'd been experiencing.

It was still approximately nine minutes before ten, the sign-off time, when Bob said: "You know Sid. We should pull a trick on our fellow friend and neighbor, Dale." Dale owned and operated the funeral home directly across the street from our house.

I brightened at the prospect. "Do you have any ideas, Bob?"

"Can't you pull his leg with a funny telephone call?" Bob suggested. "You do fake voices really well."

"Yaah, let me think." A funny scenario popped into my head and I started laughing. I had a lot of recording equipment for a business that was causing me both pleasure and stress.

Why not use it in a fun way to relieve that stress? We'd reached the station by then.

I said to Bob: "When I flip this switch you'll be able to hear both sides of the conversation."

Bob was already chuckling even though he had no idea how this lark was going to unfold. "We'll use the station telephone." I said.

"When the talking starts, all I need to do is push this little button on the recorder and both sides of the conversation will be recorded." "Great" said Bob, shaking his head and grinning.

I dialed the telephone number of the funeral home. It was answered on first ring and I immediately recognized Dale's voice.

I changed my voice to a high pitch, which made it sound as if I were a nervous, agitated female, with a thick foreign accent.

"This is Mrs. Stowkowski from Deming. Hey do you volks half shmelling salts?"

In a calm, dignified voice Dale responded: "Yes we have smelling salts."

"Oh, tad's gud. I want me husband to pick up sum shmellin salts".

"We don't normally sell smelling salts," answered Dale, "what do you need them for, Mrs Slow . . ."

"Oh it's my cussin Lukey," I interrupted. "He's dead and he dun shmell so good no more."

Maintaining his calm, professional funeral home voice Dale said: "Your cousin Lukey died at home? Did you call a doctor?"

"No, I didn't call a doctor. Lukey is dead and my husband wants to bury him under the hen house."

Dale said, "I'm sorry your cousin died."

"Dat's OK," I interrupted, squeekier and louder. "Lukey never did amount to a hill of beans anyvay."

Out of the corner of my eye I could see Bob valiantly struggling to keep from exploding into laughter. He knew that if he made noise, Dale would be able to hear that because I was using the studio microphone to talk on the telephone. If Dale heard laughter in the background he would immediately know that it was a "crank call."

Bob bounded from his chair. His face contorted and beet red with compressed laughter, he quickly fled the confines of the small studio into an adjoining part of the building. He soon returned not wanting to miss anything.

Again Dale asked if the doctor had been called. He got the same high-pitched response: "Lukey is dead, doctor not can help Lukey no more."

Dale went into a calm, reasoned explanation why the law requires that authorities be called whenever someone dies at home without the presence of a physician.

I simply pretended not to understand any of that. As Bob had re-appeared in the doorway I decided to ignore completely what Dale was talking about. I was hamming it up like crazy, and Bob was a great audience. I continued in the near hysterical voice: "Shay, shay, me husband is fixing a box to put Lukey in and shuff it under de henhouse and he wonts me to aks you . . . . no . . . wait . . . . he says de box is dunn but Lukey won't fit in de box. He want me to aks you if it OK to leev de end out of de box and let Lukey's toes stick out."

Bob fled the doorway again, choking back guffaws.

I had to wait several seconds before Dale answered. I'm sure Dale had encountered pretty naïve foreigners before, but he must have been holding his own laughter. Surely this crazy female on the phone was as dumb as a rock. Still, he remained calm and dignified as he again started to explain the laws of the land pertaining to coroners, cause of death, and the requirement for a special permit if the family wanted to bury a loved anywhere outside a regular cemetery.

Again I ignored all the good advice and carried on with increasingly high-pitched excitement and urgency: "You don understand Mr. Schmelling Salts. My cousin Lukey is dead. Ve don half no money. Lukey' don half no money. He was a no gud lazy fard. All he ever dun wus milk de goat tree dimes a day. Now ve yust wan to know if OK my husband leave de end off de box so Lukey's toes stik out before he shuffs him under de henhouse."

With that whacky speech Dale lost his patience and his professional decorum. By now he was absolutely certain that the woman on the phone was a complete "fruitcake". "Yes, Mrs. Slaphorsky, or who-ever you are. Just put dead old Lukey in de box, knock the one end out so his toes stick out. Then shove him under the henhouse with his head pointing East so he'll be the first to notice the uprising when it comes."

Quickly and excitedly I shouted, "Shay . . . shay . . . me husband yust cum in and he say dat Lukey yust burped!"

With that I quickly hung up, unable to contain my own laughter any longer. I rewound the cassette audiotape with the recorded conver-sation; shut down the studio equipment the lights, locked the doors and headed along the sidewalk toward our house.

We were still nearly two blocks from 211 Front Street when we saw the familiar form of our mutual friend Dale sprinting across the street toward our house.

Later, he told us that after he replaced the phone on the cradle he had realized that this "stupid woman" from Deming had been a joke call. He knew me quite well and his intuition told him that I was the most likely culprit. Dale's and Bob's wives both joined us as we en-joyed Margaret's coffee and cake, listened to the recording of the crazy telephone conversation, courtesy of my electronics business.

We laughed till nearly midnight.

All the pressures of the day dissolved and after a good night sleep I was ready to deal with the challenges of a new day.

Terrorism in the 1960s

We had added some additional electronic equipment to our on-premises background music tape players. The systems were designed to operate in supermarkets with multiple speakers placed thru out the supermarkets. The speakers would be activated and alert the shoppers of some outstanding value of certain products featured at special prices for the next hour only. We now had a sales representative crisscrossing the United States in an effort to establish dealers in various states. Those were all ambitious ideas and activities. Our primary problem was lack of adequate capital. When a dealer ordering our equipment wasn't able to pay promptly within thirty days, we were heading for serious problems. The pressures and anxiety levels mounted. But Margaret had good news. My brother and his family were coming from Michigan to visit.

Henk and I had always been close. Even though his family now lived more than 2,000 miles away, we still managed to share some of life's experiences at least once a year. My sister Greta with husband Wayne and their family also lived in Michigan. Wayne and I hit it off from the time we first met.

Now they would be spending some vacation time with family in Washington and I definitely needed to plan a few days vacation time, which wasn't easy. Brother-in-law Wayne would visit me at my place of business, and in between answering the telephones and waiting on clients we had time to plan the next prank. When we got together for a prank brainstorming session, our plots grew increasingly elaborate.

Wayne had read in the newspaper that, as had happened a year earlier, the motorcycle gang known as Hell's Angels were planning to come to the nearby resort in Birch Bay again. "You know, Sid, we could probably pull a trick on our friend Rook and make him believe that he is being terrorized by the Hell's Angels."

Looking through our office window, Wayne pointed to where Rook was sitting in his office typing a message on the Western Union Teletype machine. "I know!" said Wayne. "We should get one of those harmless car bombs that you can wire to a spark plug and an ignition wire. When our unsuspecting victim starts his car, he'll be in for a scary surprise." Wayne leapt from his chair and as he disappeared through the door, grinning from ear to ear, he said, "I think I know where I can get one of those screaming 'smoke bombs'."

Early in the afternoon he returned, carefully hiding his most recent acquisition.

We had no idea how we could ignite this modified "bottle rocket" while it was inside a teletype machine without the operator noticing. I asked our most creative electronic technician to get in on our brainstorming sessions. It didn't take Steve very long to come up with a plan that would allow for the remotely activated detonation of the explosive device we planned to hide inside the Teletype machine. Steve assured us that he'd probably have to work at it all night but he would get it done.

We had a busy, fun-filled evening, strategizing our plans to pull a scary prank on my friend and business associate Rook.

The following morning we learned that Steve had installed the "bomb" in the Teletype machine with remote activation from our electronic service department in the rear of the building. It was time to implement all the details Wayne and I had strategized the evening before. I found time to write a brief script, which would have to be read on the telephone by someone who would pretend to be calling from the Western Union main office in Portland. Wayne wandered off and seated himself across from Rook in our Travel Agency/Western Union office, which was also a part of our business.

Wayne was born and raised in the Grand Rapids area of Michigan where Rook had also lived for a number of years before moving to Bellingham. That morning Wayne looked very serious when he said: "Rook, have you heard about the Hell's Angels at Birch Bay?"

Rooks brown eyes widened when he stopped typing and responded: "Did they arrive at Birch Bay again?"

"Yes, and you know, those gangsters are nothing but a bunch of terrorists." This was before the world became much more familiar with "terrorism" than it was in the 1960s.

"You know what they're doing?" Wayne continued. Rook's eyes grew larger still as he repositioned himself in his chair with a very serious look on his face along with an expression that reflected curiosity. He didn't even have to prompt Wayne to continue.

"Rook, I've heard that they're responsible for putting very high voltage charges on telephone lines, which has resulted in some people's telephones blowing right off the wall or exploding right on people's desks or tables."

Rook's eyes now nearly popped out of their sockets with alarm, fear and empathy reflected on his face all at the same time. "I better go listen to the radio some more", said Wayne as he exited Rook's office and told me that he had Rook properly "primed."

I let Steve read the message the "Western Union lady" needed to read after calling Rook by telephone. Steve laughed and said he was sure his mother would do that.

We discussed all the final details including how Steve would receive the message that would tell him it was time to pull the "detonation" switch. I would call Steve's mother during the afternoon, hopefully during a slow period in store traffic, to tell her that it was a good time for her to make the fateful phone call to Rook.

It was near the middle of the afternoon when hardly any customers were in the store. I quickly went into the KLYN radio studio to call Steve's mom. All the switches had been arranged that would allow Steve, in the service department, to listen to both sides of the telephone conversation. A few moments later I heard the phone ring on Rook's desk and quickly pushed a switch allowing both Steve and myself to tap into the line going into Rook's office. The female voice said: "Mr. VanHalm, this is Lucie at the head office of Western Union in Portland." She didn't pause for a response from Rook, instead quickly continuing: "We have received reports that somewhere there is a subversive organization that is placing very high voltage charges on Western Union lines resulting in Teletype machines exploding. We wanted to warn you because this could be extremely dangerous to personnel." Again without waiting for response from Rook, she continued: "Have you noticed any irregularities yet in your office?"

That was the "detonation" code word: "OFFICE." As soon as Steve heard that word he pushed the button. The results were swift and astonishing. I was looking at Rook where he could not see me. I was still listening to the phone as Rook responded with a rather calm "No." Even before the short word had completely left his lips, he stopped as he noticed a tiny curl of smoke beginning to emanate from the Teletype machine, which was no more than two feet away from the chair he was sitting on.

Even before his eyes could clearly focus on the little whiff of smoke, there was a small explosion followed by an ear splitting screaming sound coming from the machine. Rook would not be out-screamed and, still holding the phone, he yelled in a fear-filled, petrified voice: "Yyyess!" With that he threw the phone as far as he could throw it, covered his face with his arms and backed out of his small office.

All personnel in the building seemed suddenly to appear from everywhere and were all standing there laughing even before Rook had completely backed out of the confines of his small office with arms still covering his face. Completely bewildered, he caught a glimpse of all those laughing people as he was swiftly fleeing for the outside door.

"Where are you going, Rook"? I yelled. Without breaking stride he yelled back: "I'm going to run down the street to get the fire department." Hearing the gathered crowd laughing hysterically, he suddenly stopped. Totally bewildered, he suddenly stopped and quickly looked at all the laughing faces. Angrily he stomped his foot on the floor and yelled, "This is no joke", as he pointed to the still smoking Teletype machine. Again looking at the laughing people he stomped his foot on the floor once more and said: "Is this a joke?" I was right beside him now and said: "Yes, Rook, this is a joke."

Still unbelieving, he pointed again to the Teletype machine where flames were now visible through the cloud of smoke. The roll of paper in the machine had actually caught on fire and someone quickly grabbed a fire extinguisher to put out the fire.

It really was a cruel joke, but Rook, Wayne, myself and probably everyone who witnessed it that day would frequently retell the story over the next forty years. Laughter being the best medicine, it may have healed many maladies and reduced many of life's stresses.

"My car is not for sale"

Yes, plotting and scheming mischief was a pastime both brother-in-law Wayne and I enjoyed. That smoky prank on Rook was just the tip of the practical-joke iceberg!

Here's another one that should amuse:

Once there was a family reunion party at my mother's house on Front Street in Lynden, scheduled for the evening.

It was during the late afternoon that Wayne entered the front door of my business at 525 Front Street. By the look on his face I could tell an imp was whispering in his ear. He was in the early stages of hatching a plan for that evening's, er, family entertainment.

"Sid," he said, "I just visited our brother-in-law Barney."

He told me about a very crazy and annoying problem Barney was dealing with that day. It was a Wednesday, which was the day the weekly local newspaper was delivered to its subscribers. Somehow, someone had placed a classified ad under "Automobiles for Sale by Owner." An ad for a 1955 Chevrolet four-door car listed the telephone number of Barney's brother. It was never determined who had placed the prank classified ad, but Barney's brother was very sure that his shiny 1955 Chevy was not for sale. And he definitely had not placed the ad. Barney said that his brother had been getting calls all afternoon and he was just getting sick of having to explain that his car was not for sale. He had even called The Lynden

Tribune. All they could tell him that someone had placed the ad and paid cash in advance.

The seed for a prank had unwittingly been planted.

Seated as family around the dinner table at my mother's house that evening, Barney told the whole family about his brother's woes all because of a "car for sale" ad that he had not placed. Suddenly Wayne's eyes lit up. "Sid, you should call him up and pretend you want to buy the car."

Barney was snickering. He had heard all about poor old Lukey under the henhouse. He too was encouraging me to call his brother. After a few minutes of mentally planning the conversation I dialed the number. "Hello." It was answered on the third ring. Again squeezing my voice to the highest possible pitch I said: "Is this 354-1234?"

"Yes," came the somewhat tentative response. "This is Mrs. Stowkowski from Sedro-Woolley. Ve see your ad in de paper. Ve only have a small motorcycle. We are getting on in years and me hosband tink ve shud git a car. Can ve buy your car?"

The response was a firm "No" to which I responded with a lengthy loud sigh, which left no doubt as to the depth of "Mrs. Stowkowski's" disappointment. After hearing my disappointment, so sadly expressed, Barney's brother's voice softened and he patiently explained that he had not placed the ad in the Tribune, that he did not want to sell his car and that the whole thing was a mistake.

I pretended not to really understand what he was talking about and decided to begin explaining our great need for a car. "See, ve is poor folk. Ve haf a few chickens, a hog and two goats. Every two veeks me hosband get feed for dem animals. Last time de hole bag of chicken feed felt off de motorbike. It busted open and all de corn all over de place. He only saved a few hands full and put that in his pockets. Me poor hosband was bawling ven he get home. See ve need something wit four wheels and ve have de money for your car."

"Lady, I don't want to sell my car. You should call one of the other advertisements in the paper." With that he hung up the phone.

The family, all-sitting around the table, had been stifling their laughter even though they could only hear my side of the conversation. Now laughter burst forth in waves until Wayne loudly called my sister Mary's name.

"Mary, you should call Barney's brother and pretend you are an operator from the telephone company." At that time any long distance calls were routed through an operator in the telephone company office.

Mary quickly captured the idea and was already dialing.

"Sir, did you just receive a long distance call from Sedro-Woolley?"

"Yes, I did."

"The party that called does not have an account with the telephone company and I will have to reverse the charges to your account."

Our poor victim had nearly come unglued. He went into a lengthy, agitated explanation that she should charge it to The Lynden Tribune. He should not be responsible for any costs resulting from an ad he had never placed.

"Well, sir," Mary responded in a very official-sounding telephone operator voice, "you will have to take that up with The Lynden Tribune."

She hung up and it was time to let laughter have its way again.

Then it was time for me to call our victim again and inform him that I couldn't afford the other cars advertised. I could hear the agitation and weariness in his voice when he answered.

I raised my voice about two octaves before I said, "This is Mrs. Stowkowski. Ve really want to buy your. . . . ."

"Lady, listen," he interrupted. "I am sick and tired of this. I've been on the phone all day long. You even charged your phone call to me. I'm so mad I can't see straight. And by golly, my car is not for sale. How often do I have to tell you?"

I could tell he was really very angry and understandably very frustrated. I decided there was only one way an old lady could calm a man's anger. In a high-pitched voice I started wailing and wailing in desperate tones until I heard, "I'm sorry, lady, I didn't mean to make you cry. This mess really isn't your fault at all."

Ah, good, I thought. There's nothing that weakens a man's resolve like an old lady's tears.

With a tear-laden high-pitched voice, I said, "Ve vould like to cum look at de car tomorrow. I vill ride wit me hosband on de back of de motorbike."

His compassion for a poor crying old lady simply did not allow him to refuse.

Emboldened now, I carried on.

"Say, ve probably won't get there till close to suppertime. Is it Okay if ve stay fur supper?"

He meekly agreed and I decided to plow ahead.

"Then it vill soon be dark and ve don' have light on de old motorbike. Is it all right that ve stay overnight?"

This pushed him over the edge again and he literally screamed, "Lady, we don't have an extra bed!" I resorted promptly to the mournful wails again and screeched, "That's Okay, me husband and me can sleep on de couch." He wearily agreed. I replaced the telephone in its cradle and turned to look at the family members. All exploded again in waves of laughter they had only barely been able to suppress.

It was, at times, even with a little sympathy, that we reflected on the emotional trauma we were placing upon our poor victim. We all knew him and liked him very well and certainly didn't want to make him suffer. But oh, the laughter was so healthy.

Suddenly, Wayne sat straight up in his chair already grinning about his plan.

"You know, Barney's brother has agreed for the old folks from Sedro-Woolley to come and look at his car. He'll even put them up overnight. He already knows that old lady has the money. He'll probably cave in and sell his car. But he probably doesn't really know what his car is really worth. I'm going to call him." With that he picked up the receiver and dialed the local number.

"Hello, sorry to call you so late in the evening but I just noticed your ad in the paper about selling your car. My name is Sam. I'm the sales manager at Hinton Chevrolet here in Lynden and I can guarantee that I can give you a lot more money on trade-in than anybody would pay you for it." He didn't give our poor victim a chance to respond and carried on without a pause.

"I've got a beauty on our lot and I'd like to drive it over to your place tomorrow and show you. I know you'll be very surprised to find out what your car is really worth."

This time there was no long explanation about the mistaken ad, the Tribune and the endless phone calls. It simply remained silent for a few moments. Wayne could hear the breathing in the phone. "Well, I have some people coming over from Sedro-Woolley and it would be good if I knew what my car was worth."

"Great, I'll bring it over tomorrow. It's really a beauty; you can test drive it and take your wife for a little ride around town. It'll probably be close to noon before I can get over there and your wife wouldn't mind if I stayed for a little lunch, would she?"

"No, that should be all right."

"Great, I'll see you tomorrow."

It was nearly noon the following day when Wayne strolled into our store. He placed himself on a chair by the telephone and, grinning from ear to ear, was dialing a number.

Curious whom he was calling, I hovered near him and heard him say: "Hello, this is Sam from Hinton's. I'm on my way. In fact I'm calling from your neighbor's house only about a half mile from your place. For some reason my car quit. I'm sure it's just some little thing. I wonder if you could come with your tractor and pull me on your yard. You'll see me as soon as you drive out of your driveway."

"Okay. I'll be right there."

Again, my stomach ached with laughter. We did not want to reveal our identity and did not check to see the big farm tractor pull out of the driveway.

To this day, none of the participants have dared to admit to their friend and brother that they were responsible for that cruel joke.

The Poisonous Prolix

One of my pranks got me in big trouble.

It had been a very busy day. Snow had been in the weather forecasts for the past two days and many people were coming into town to stock up on their needs. I looked out of the large store window. There was a thermometer at the service station across the street and it had just dipped below thirty degrees. The wind had shifted to the northeast and increased in velocity. As I loaded our remote broadcast equipment in the van, I looked up at the sky. The dark cloud layer looked heavy laden but it hadn't started snowing yet. Basketball games in the county had not been cancelled. Tonight was the big game between cross-town rivals Lynden and Lynden Christian High Schools. Radio station KLYN-FM broadcast every Lynden and Lynden Christian game as they played against other Whatcom county teams. I simply had to gather our remote broadcast equipment and bring it to the school where the game was scheduled. When our sports-announcing team arrived, they would be able to quickly establish a test connection with our studio. I was not the sports announcer. In fact, I had great admiration for Terry DeValois and Tony Mellema, both of whom had the skills to carry on rapid-fire descriptions of the play-by-play of a fast-moving basketball game. When a referee blew the whistle, they often knew in advance which player had committed an infraction.

The broadcast booth provided a good view of all the action on the floor, and I never needed to worry about finding a place to sit. Tonight my brother-in-law Perry and his wife were coming to our house. Perry and I would go to the game together. As we headed to the high school a little after seven, the northeast wind had dramatically increased in velocity and I noticed snowflakes speedily heading downwind. Perry said, "You know, Sid, in Birch Bay it's been snowing and blowing most of the day already. One of our drivers nearly got stuck in a snowdrift at about five o'clock, and this evening all roads in the Blaine-Birch Bay area are closed as a result of huge snowdrifts."

Birch Bay is about twelve miles west of Lynden, I responded, "That's unusual, Perry. It usually is a lot worse around here before it gets bad in Blaine and Birch Bay."

As I pulled into the school parking lot Perry said, "I'm afraid we're in for a pack of snow here too. It could look pretty bad by tomorrow."

"Yes, we might all be snowed in by tomorrow," I said.

We shoved our hands deep in our pockets and braved the elements of nature as we headed for the heated gymnasium.

After a close and exciting basketball game, we headed back to the warmth of our home.

It was really snowing hard now and the wind was blowing even harder. Snowdrifts were already in the making and they would surely grow. "Sid, I've heard about some of the crazy telephone calls you've been making," said Perry. "Well, yes, Perry, but they put me up to it. Do you have a victim in mind?"

"I'd sure like you to pull a good joke on my partner Ernie, Sid. He had one of our drivers deliver a tank of Prolix dairy nutrients to a good customer in Birch Bay yesterday. It's a good thing he did. He wouldn't be able to get there now, what with the snow, and the Malcolms are not very patient, but are very good customers. I mean they buy a lot of dairy feeds from us."

"Ok, let me see if I can dream up some kind of crazy scenario," I said as I parked the car in front of our house. "Tell me all about Prolix, Perry. Does it come in bags, in barrels, or what?"

"No Sid. It's a liquid. It has practically every nutrient recommended for dairy cows and they love it. It's kind of like syrup."

"How do you feed syrup to a cow, Perry"?

"Oh, we pour it into a special Prolix tank that we supply to all our customers."

"That still doesn't explain how the farmer gets the syrup into the cow."

"Sure, I see what you mean. The big Prolix tank has a drum that begins to rotate as the cows lick it. It rotates through the syrupy liquid as long as the cows keep licking."

A picture began to emerge in my mind. "Do the Malcolms have any kids?"

"They have a little girl and a boy of about ten or eleven."

We were sitting in our living room now. The wind was really howling outside now. It was warm and cozy inside. A grin crossed my face as I looked at Perry. "I think I've got it. What's your partner's telephone number?" I walked over to the telephone in the kitchen. Perry followed. I had to work up the courage and get in the right mood, but I went ahead and dialed the phone. The call was answered on the second ring. A deep male voice said, "Hello."

I was committed now. There was no turning back.

I raised the pitch of my voice and tried to sound hysterical and breathless. I must have sounded like a lady who was chin-deep in desperate agony.

"This is Mrs. Malcolm from Birch Bay. . . . something terrible has happened here. Do you have insurance?"

"Wha . . . what happened, Mrs. Malcolm?"

Immediately I could tell that Ernie was excited and worried. Undoubtedly the "insurance" question raised the specter of liability in his mind, so I probably already had him on the ropes. Half crying, I yelled into Ernie's ear, "Oh, it's awful. Our little Timmy fell into the Prolix tank. He swallowed it and he's sicker than a dog."

Ernie excitedly interrupted me, "Mrs. Malcolm, have you called a doctor? We'll pay for it."

"Yah, we've called two doctors, we've called an ambulance, but nobody wants to come out with the slippery roads in this blizzard. My boy might die!"

I could tell Ernie was really getting excited and concerned now. "Is your boy conscious?" he asked, with noticeable fear in his voice.

"Ya, Timmy is still conscious but he's throwing up all over."

"Oh, my," Ernie responded. He was clearly falling for the hoax and I needed to make it a bit more ridiculous.

"He's not just throwing up; he's got a terrible case of diarrhea. It's coming out everywhere. I don't have a clean towel left."

"Don't worry, Mrs. Malcolm. We'll bring you some clean towels. . . ." I interrupted him, virtually crying at the top of my lungs. "Oh, no. Oh no! My husband just came into the house with a b . . . b . . . baseball bat. He . . . he . . . he k-k-killed the cow that peed in the Prolix tank. Oooooh . . . ooooooh!"

Perry was standing only six feet behind me, stifling his laughter. Now he fled down the stairs that led into our basement. I heard the muffled sounds of him exploding with pent-up guffaws.

I'm sure if Ernie, only for a moment, had been able to get the fear of liability exposure out of his head, he would have realized that this was just an outrageously impossible hoax. But he couldn't. Instead, he said with an anxiety-laden voice, "I'll call my partner Perry. We'll dig my car out of the driveway. We'll fill it with towels and be on our way. Is there anything else you need, Mrs. Malcolm?"

Still hysterical, I answered, "Yes, all my bedding, sheets, pillows and blankets are an unbelievable stinking mess. Boooh . . . ooooh."

"Don't worry," answered Ernie. "I'll load the car with blankets, sheets, towels and soap. Is there anything else you need?"

Frantically, I tried to think of something sufficiently insane that Ernie would stop and say, "Hey, what is this?" Then it came to me. This would certainly get the fear of liability out of his head and make him realize that someone was jerking his chain big time.

Continuing in my high-pitched, urgent voice, I said, "Yes, when I opened the refrigerator door earlier, to get some salve for Timmy's inflamed rear-end, all my breakfast eggs fell out and broke on the floor." Now I could hardly contain my own laughter as I envisioned this totally crazy imaginary scenario at the Malcolm home in Birch Bay. I waited for Ernie to burst out laughing, so he wouldn't have to get his car ready to drive to Birch Bay this snowy evening. I just couldn't let him do that. He had told Mrs. Malcolm that he was going to call his partner Perry to help. Well, Perry had come forth out of the basement again and was just inches from where I was standing. Now he was fleeing again when he heard me ask Ernie to bring some breakfast eggs to replace the ones that had broken on account of Timmy Malcolm's inflamed rear. Of course, he couldn't hear Ernie's side of the conversation and he didn't know that even that final request for him to bring some eggs did nothing to discourage Ernie from promising Mrs. Malcolm that he would be on his way soon, eggs and all.

After hanging up it was time to release all the pent-up laughter. We told our wives and enjoyed a barrel of laughs.

"Perry," I said, "Ernie is going to call you, but you're not home. He won't be able to get hold of you. We really can't let him brave the blizzard and slippery roads to try to get to Birch Bay. And should he succeed and make it to the Malcolm farm, he'd really look foolish."

"Don't worry Sid," Perry responded. "We were talking about the ballgame tonight and I told him that we were going to your place and that you and I would go to the game together."

Not three minutes later the phone rang. Margaret answered. It was for Perry.

As Ernie excitedly told him about the catastrophe at the Malcolm farm and that they needed to go over to Birch Bay immediately, Perry listened quietly. Then I heard him say "Ernie, that call you got was Sid." Ernie didn't hear what Perry was saying. He was so wound up that twice more he told Perry how urgent the situation was and twice more Perry told him that Sid had played a joke on him. Midway to reiterating the Malcolm's plight for a third time, he stopped in mid-sentence. Slowly he said, "What. Did. You. Say?"

"Ernie, that was Sid. He was just pulling your leg."

There was stunned silence before Ernie slowly said, "I'm. Going. To. Wring. Sid's. Neck."

Ernie and I continued to be good friends, but I stayed out of his way for quite a long time after that.

From Prank to Panic

Three thousand feet below us, the green fertile farmlands of Skagit County, Washington, slowly receded below the wheels of the small, four-place Piper Tri-Pacer. We were heading south. My brother Henry was doing the flying from the copilot's seat. My sons Jim and Jerry were enjoying the scenic beauty of the Northwest from the back seat. The boys were approaching their teenage years and I knew that soon carefree outings with "old dad" would no longer be a desirable priority in their lives.

The purpose of our mission was to deliver posters to other airport offices promoting the upcoming breakfast fly-in and air show at the Lynden airport.

We were approaching the Snohomish County airport, better known as Paine Field, near the city of Everett.

I pushed the talk switch on the microphone and said, "Paine tower, this is Piper November (N) 2334 Alpha (A) at 3000 inbound for Kitsap County airport, request clearance to transit Paine control area at 3000."

The controller responded almost immediately. "Piper November 2334 Alpha, cleared to transit Paine airspace at 3000, remain West of extended runway 16."

"Roger Paine tower. Piper 34 Alpha is cleared to transit Paine airspace remaining west of extended runway 16."

Smoothly we droned toward our first destination with Henry at the controls.

This was a good time to make sure he wouldn't fall asleep. I put my arms behind me and stretched holding the back of my head with hands clasped. Unobtrusively I could now reach the small zippered control cable pulley inspection pocket. I grabbed the cable firmly between thumb and finger and gave it a good yank. The airplane responded immediately by banking the right wing very abruptly and not altogether gently.

Henry's eyes bugged out. He jerked the control wheel to the neutral position again and yelled, "What was that?"

I pretended to be alarmed as well and with a completely serious expression on my face simply shrugged my shoulders. Whatever it had been, all went smoothly again. It was time for another relaxing stretch. This time I pulled the opposite cable and the airplane suddenly banked violently to the left. With great alarm Henry yelled, "Sid, you take the airplane."

I couldn't contain my laughter anymore. For a moment Henk, uncomprehending, stared at me. Then, with disgust in his voice, he said, "Did you do that?"

I nodded and couldn't stop laughing while I showed my brother how I had been able to make that airplane behave so erratically. Now he grinned, just slightly, as he took control of the airplane again. The scenery below was absolutely beautiful. The visibility was limited only by the curvature of the earth and distant horizons. The snowcapped Olympic Mountain range sparkled like huge diamonds to the West, with Mount Rainier and the Cascade mountains dominating the scenery to the east. The vast metropolitan area of Seattle was gliding by below and to the left of the pilot seat.

I checked the back seat. Jimmy was looking at the Seattle skyscrapers, which seemed so insignificant now. It was hard to imagine that those buildings were the same as the huge structures that, when viewed from the inside of our red Ford station wagon, dwarfed surrounding roads, cars, and buildings. The constant droning of the Tri-Pacer engine was conducive to slumber and Jerry had given in to a little nap.

"Kitsap County traffic, this is Piper 2334 Alpha, approaching from the north at 3000, inbound for Kitsap County Airport, landing on 34."

There was no tower control at our first destination and I was only required to announce our presence and intentions to possible other airplanes landing or flying in the vicinity of the airport.

A few minutes later we touched down smoothly on runway 34. There was a strong breeze from the North, which determined the runway to be used. The heading for runway 34 was only 20 degrees to the left of straight north.

We dropped a poster off with the friendly people in the airport base operations office and taxied out for takeoff. Soon we were climbing in a northeasterly direction with the intention of making the airport at Bellevue, which has since closed, our next destination. We never made it.

A strong headwind from the northeast slowed our progress as the airplane engine labored to gain altitude. Brother Henry was flying again while I continued to scan the skies and the instruments.

Suddenly there was a sharp jolt, combined with what sounded like a mini explosion in the engine. Instantly the windshield was covered with oil. The engine RPMs dropped to about half and all the beauty that had surrounded us suddenly vanished in a sea of fear and anxiety. Henk immediately turned the controls over to me. We were clearly experiencing a serious emergency. I watched the oil pressure gauge drop to zero and the engine temperature climb rapidly to the red line marking on the gauge. I looked down for a suitable emergency-landing site. I turned the airplane 180 degrees and saw the airport from which we had departed only minutes before. We were losing altitude now, and we would not be able to return to a nice concrete runway. There was nothing but thickly wooded gently rolling hill country below. No nice pastureland anywhere within gliding distance. The boys in the back seat were anxious to know what was happening. I calmly told them that we were going to land again. From training I remembered that panicking pilots are perilous.

The engine clunked and coughed. With each clunk I expected it to quit completely. The cockpit filled with the acrid smell of burning oil. The temperature gauge was pinned beyond the red line. I saw no clearing within gliding distance where a landing could be attempted with a reasonable chance of survival.

After reversing our direction, the strong headwind immediately became a strong tailwind, boosting our forward speed by at least 25 MPH. The runway from which we had departed didn't seem so far away anymore. I prayed that the stricken engine would keep sputtering at half its normal RPMs just a little longer. If so, it would allow me to glide the remaining distance to the runway.

There was no conversation, only white knuckles.

Then I keyed the microphone and announced, "Kitsap traffic, Piper 2334 Alpha, three miles north on extended final for emergency landing downwind, runway 16."

Any airplane departing from the opposite end of the runway would be on a direct collision course with our airplane. The announcement on the communications radio should have alerted all active airplanes near the airport that we had an emergency situation. It felt as though we held our collective breaths for the next several minutes, ground coming up slowly beneath us, until the tires contacted the asphalt runway. The engine sputtered its final cough. I steered the coasting airplane onto the grass, just off the runway.

It would be many weeks before the Tri-Pacer had a new engine and was ready to fly again.

What should have been a wonderfully relaxing day had turned into a day of enormous stress and disaster potential. It was time to chase the effects of stress with fun and laughter.

Terrorism in Michigan

My wife Margaret always played a critical support role in all my businesses.

She did accounts payable and payroll for the Electronics and Music store, for Lynden Travel Agency, for radio station KLYN-FM, and for Motivating Sound, Inc.

It wasn't easy to find a few days in any month when we could feel comfortable planning a little vacation. It wasn't easy to plan a nearly one-week trip to Michigan. But we had close family members there. Brother Henry with his wife Ruth and family lived in Grand Rapids. Sister Greta and her husband Wayne and family lived in Hudsonville. We could not continue to ignore their reminders that it was way past time for us to schedule a return visit.

Margaret said, "Honey, if we're ever going to get to Michigan, it has to be between the 15th and 25th day of the month. I checked with two of my sisters and they can take care of the kids from the 18th to the 25th."

"Okay, let's do it," I responded, knowing that for a whole week I would have to delegate numerous business activities and responsibilities to others. Looking at each other from facing seats in the train, we sighed heavily and let our shoulders sag, hardly believing that we were finally going to take a vacation with family in Michigan. It wasn't my nature to idly stare out of the window and let the beautiful landscapes unfold before my eyes. Relaxation wasn't part of my lexicon, and soon I immersed myself in studying for my First Class FCC license. As the owner and licensee of a broadcasting station I was required to have a technician on the payroll who held a First Class FCC license and could at all times verify and document that our transmitter equipment was operating within allowable tolerance levels. Financially I could not afford to add another employee to the KLYN-FM payroll. The radio station wasn't even breaking even yet and a person holding a first class F.C.C. license was entitled to above average pay. I just didn't have the money. That was the reason I spent every idle moment with the complicated technical study material. I simply needed to pass the FCC test and would then qualify to add another responsibility to my long roster. In addition to station owner, general manager, program manager, talk show host, I would also be the station's first class engineer. It was simply an economic necessity for the survival of the station.

When we rolled into the train station in Grand Rapids, I closed the book and promised Margaret not to open it again as long as we were in Michigan.

We had a wonderful dinner with family that evening. Brother-in-law Wayne related the tale of the "Hells Angels" exploding the poor travel agent's Teletype machine. Once again, all the laughter banished my pent-up accumulated stresses.

My sister Greta suddenly got an inspiration. "You know what, Sid? We have big Dave at our house. You're going to have to play a trick on him." Just the thought of it caused Wayne to burst forth with laughter, all the while nodding his head vigorously to indicate his complete approval of Greta's idea.

"Who's Dave?" I asked.

Greta explained that Dave was from Texas. He was in his early twenties and the Bakers had been asked to expose Dave, for a period of time, to a loving, functional Christian home environment. If there was an opportunity to help others, Wayne and Greta Baker were always ready. They knew so well that a key ingredient of a great functional family home life was much fun and laughter. This time they wanted Dave to be the catalyst.

"Dave is a big strong guy", explained Wayne. "He's as harmless as a loaf of Wonder bread but wouldn't score 100 on an IQ test. You'll be staying at our house tonight. I'm sure you can dream up something."

Oh, my goodness, here I had come to completely relax and now they wanted me to come up with something to rattle big Dave's cage. I made no promises, even though my mind immediately went into action running through various scenarios.

Soon we arrived at the spacious new home of Wayne and Greta Baker. Music was playing in every room. "We have a central intercom-radio music system," Wayne explained as he showed us around the house, "with wall-mounted speakers in every room. The main unit is in the kitchen, and when Greta has dinner ready, she simply presses a button on the main unit, which activates the intercom. That way, wherever the kids are in the house, she can call them to come to dinner, lunch, and breakfast."

Wayne continued. "I know Dave's favorite radio station is playing. I'm sure he's in his bedroom listening. I'll ask him to come out so you can meet him."

Dave appeared shortly after Wayne called him. He was indeed a strong, husky young man with a gentle face and manner. We smiled warmly as we shook hands. He seemed shy and somewhat uncomfortable, and he soon excused himself, saying that he was going back to bed.

That radio-intercom system intrigued me. "Wayne?" I asked. "Do you have to switch from radio to intercom mode whenever you want to make an announcement?"

"No," he responded. "Whenever you press the intercom lever it automatically silences the radio."

That answered my question and I said, "Okay, I have an idea."

I asked Wayne a number of questions about names of nearby roads, highways, and other landmarks. Then I said, "Dave is obviously listening to the radio. He'll hear any announcements. Should Dave come out of bed again, make sure you look serious. Don't let on that a joke is in progress."

They were grinning as I headed for the control unit in the kitchen.

In the middle of a musical selection played by the radio station, I squeezed the button that turned on intercom mode. Without any clicks it instantly silenced the radio program and in my best radio announcer voice I said:

"We interrupt this program to bring you a special emergency message from the Michigan State Patrol. Two males, driving an older pickup truck were heading East on 17th Avenue when they detonated what appears to have been a nuclear explosive in the vicinity of Grandville. Preliminary reports indicate widespread damage with numerous casualties. We now return to our regular programming. You are requested to remain tuned for further information and directives from the Michigan State Patrol. We now return you to our regular programming."

I released the pushbutton switch, and all the home speakers continued playing the radio music while I quickly returned to join Margaret, Greta and Wayne in the living room.

They were all grinning.

Wayne shook his head. "Boy, that sounded real. I almost began to believe it myself."

With that the door flew open and big Dave stood there barefooted, half dressed and trembling. His eyes were wide open with fear. "Did you hear that?" he asked, looking at our very serious faces. Wayne, acting nervous said: "Dave, don't turn that radio off. I think I actually heard and felt it some fifteen minutes ago. I'm sure there's more information coming."

A few minutes, after Dave returned to his bedroom, there it was again:

"We interrupt this program to bring you the following emergency information from the Michigan State Patrol. The Michigan State Office of Emergency Management urges all residents who have survived the explosion of a nuclear-like device living within a three-mile radius of the corner of 17th Ave. and Grandville Street to evacuate immediately. The devastation is catastrophic. Many homes and farms are ablaze. Livestock were blown out of the pastureland and some cows are dangling across high voltage lines. Those living within a ten-mile radius of the area are requested to remain fully dressed and be prepared for immediate evacuation, pending assessment of possible radiation levels. We now return to our regular programming."

It was hard to keep straight faces when Dave appeared in the living room again, nervously asking, "Do we have to evacuate?"

With a straight face, Wayne replied, "We may well have to, Dave. Better put all your clothes on, including your boots. Keep it all on when you go to bed."

Dave quickly returned to the bedroom to get fully dressed. Greta and Margaret were virtually choking with pent-up laughter.

A few minutes later Wayne said: "Let's go check on Dave."

We walked to his bedroom. The door was open and his radio speaker was turned extra loud. Fully clothed, wearing knee-high boots, he lay on his bed.

"Dave," said Wayne, "let's take a look outside. See if we can see the fires in the distance."

We looked in the direction where the announcements had indicated the explosions occurred and Wayne pointed to an area where some light from a heavy commercial area reflected against the dark night sky.

Later I learned that the power of suggestion had caused Dave to see the lighted sky differently than it truly was. He even imagined seeing flames like huge fingers pointing skyward.

Through the open window we could still hear Dave's bedroom radio speaker.

I quietly slipped in the house again. A little earlier I had asked Wayne about the names of Dave's closest friend living in the "affected" area.

Nobody could see me when I pushed the intercom button again. "We interrupt this program to bring you the following emergency report as issued by the Michigan State Patrol," I intoned gravely. "Blodget General Hospital in Grand Rapids has just released the names of the first fatalities. Wiesel Von Goldshmitt, Barney VanderGoogle, and Sander Smits. Please stay tuned. We now return to our regular programming."

Dave had moved close to his bedroom window as soon as he heard another announcement being broadcast. Now he completely lost what had been a rather stoic demeanor. "My friend Sander is dead!" he cried.

Quickly Wayne turned around and without saying anything entered the house.

I was still at the main control unit when I pushed the button again. "Ladies and gentlemen. This is radio station BLNY in Grand Rapids informing you with profound apologies that a former employee in our technical department during the past half hour has squelched the broadcast signal from this station and instead inserted a spurious, scary, and totally erroneous announcement. This cruel prank has undoubtedly caused fear, stress, and panic among our listeners and we express our deepest regrets. The culprit has now been caught and you can rest peacefully and safely tonight as we return to our regular programming."

Within seconds Dave stormed into the living room, complete in overcoat and boots.

"Did you hear that?" he yelled. We solemnly nodded our heads. "Oh boy," Dave continued, "If I got my hands on the bastard who did that, I'd drape his naked body across a pair of high voltage lines and fry him!"

Fortunately for yours truly, Dave never did learn the identity of the cruel "announcer."

No Drivers License

She had been laughing for minutes.

Finally, she got control of herself, holding her sides as though they were aching from her mirth.

"Uncle Sid!" Meribeth called from across the lunch table at Russ's Restaurant, where most of our Grand Rapids area family— nieces and nephews and cousins—had gathered.

Most of them were doubled over with laughter, as Wayne and Greta told them about the joke I had just played on their poor big Dave the night before.

The story came in bits and pieces, interrupted by the laughter.

"Uncle Sid?" It was our niece Meribeth Baker again, the beautiful daughter of Wayne and Greta.

By the look on her face I could tell that she was excited about something. She looked at me with a broad and beautiful but somewhat naughty smile.

This time she got my attention and I yelled across the table, which was lined on both sides with happy, laughing relatives.

"Yes, Meribeth?"

I answered loudly, because if I were to hear what Meribeth wanted to say I needed everyone to be quiet.

"Uncle Sid, I have a girlfriend in the senior class at high school who's never been asked out on a date. She has a crush on a boy named

Billy, but he never asks her out. Billy's also a senior and a pretty good student, but he's very shy and quiet. I'd like to play a trick on her."

"What's your girlfriend's name, Meribeth?" I asked.

"Believe it or not, her name is Meribeth too! She has a part time job at Butchar's Bakery," she said. Then she continued. "Could you call her at the bakery and pretend you're Billy and ask her for a date?" she asked.

"She'll be able to tell that it's not Billy's voice."

"I don't think she's ever really heard Billy's voice, because he's quiet and keeps to himself," she responded. "He's good looking, though."

"What's Billy's last name?" I asked. She started laughing.

"Uncle Sid, he has a strange sounding last name and he's probably self conscious about his name."

"What is it?" I asked with growing curiosity.

"His name is Billy Goad."

I chuckled.

"Okay, Meribeth, I'll try to think of a way to impersonate Billy Goad."

At about 4:30 in the afternoon Meribeth reminded me that her friend started her job at the bakery every afternoon at 4 o'clock. She also informed me that when Billy *did* talk, he talked unusually slowly. Still, he was bright and nearly always achieved straight A's on his written tests.

My niece was far more confident that I would succeed in playing a successful trick on her namesake girlfriend than I was. She was giggling constantly at the thought of her friend finally getting asked for a date.

Reminding myself to talk slow, I finally mustered sufficient courage to dial Butchers Bakery.

A friendly, youthful sounding female voice answered cheerfully: "Good evening, this is Butchar's Bakery. May I help you?"

It was very likely my target but I couldn't be sure. I had to be sure.

"Could . . . I . . . talk . . . to . . . Meribeth . . . please?"

"This is Meribeth," was the response.

"Oh . . . hi . . . Meribeth. . . . this . . . is . . . Billy . . . Goad. . . . I . . . wondered . . . if . . . I . . . could . . . take . . . you . . . to . . . dinner . . . tomorrow . . . evening."

For a few moments there was silence on the other end. It made me a little nervous.

"Well, thank you, Billy. How nice of you to call."

I breathed a silent sigh of relief. She obviously believed that she was talking to the real Billy Goad and that gave me courage.

"What . . . time . . . do . . . you . . . get . . . off . . . work . . . Meribeth?"

"I'm usually finished just a couple of minutes past six."

"Okay, Meribeth . . . I'll be . . . there . . . at . . . about . . . six . . . and . . . maybe . . . we . . . can . . . walk . . . to . . . a . . . nearby . . . restaurant".

"You have a car, don't you, Billy? I've seen you in your nice car at school."

"Yes, I have . . . car . . . but I. . . . lost . . . my . . . driver . . . license . . . for . . . six . . . months. I . . . will . . . be . . . coming . . . on . . . my . . . bicycle."

Again, there were some awkward moments of silence while niece Meribeth was struggling mightily to suppress loud laughter.

Then the Meribeth at Butchar's Bakery asked: "How come you lost your license, Billy?"

She probably thought Billy had been caught driving while intoxicated. She surely shouldn't be thinking of "her Billy" as a drunk. I would quickly dispel such possible speculation in the young lady's mind.

"Meribeth . . . they . . . took . . . my . . . license . . . away . . . because . . . I . . . ran over . . . a . . . duck."

Again, moments of silence. I watched my niece Meribeth fleeing the room. She simply couldn't contain a spontaneous combustion of laughter any longer. I could hear her in the next room. Not for long, however. She covered her mouth and quickly returned, not wanting to miss any part of the conversation with her girlfriend.

My prospective date at the bakery soon broke the silence and said with a voice clearly reflecting incredulity, "You lost your driver's license because you ran over a duck?" she asked. I could understand that it really wasn't believable, so I quickly added, "A . . . lady . . . was . . . carrying . . . the . . . duck." That was too much for my niece and she stormed out of the room again. I could hear her howling laughter in the next room, where the rest of the family was sitting.

My "date" was silent again; probably trying to visualize Billy Goad running over a duck a lady was carrying. I quickly continued.

"I'll . . . be . . . there . . . on . . . my . . . bicycle . . . about . . . 6 . . . o'clock. You . . . can . . . ride . . . with . . . me . . . on . . . the . . . bike . . . between . . . the . . . seat . . . and . . . the . . . handlebar . . . and . . . we'll . . . have . . . a . . . nice . . . dinner."

After a moment's hesitation, she said, "Okay Billy, I'll be looking for you."

The following day dawned dreary and drizzly, which wasn't typical of August Michigan weather. It was about mid-afternoon when niece Meribeth said, "Hey, Uncle Sid. A little after four, when my girlfriend is at her bakery job, I'd like to take you there so you can meet her."

"Meribeth, she's still on an emotional high anticipating her first date. And with, of all people Billy Goad, the very young man you said she had a crush on."

"Yes, Uncle Sid, but she'll be so disappointed when 6 o'clock comes and Billy doesn't show up."

"Oh, no, don't worry. I'm going to call her again at three minutes past six."

Meribeth starting laughing again and said: "Really, you're going to call her at six? What are you going to tell her?"

"I don't know yet, but I'll think of something."

She had already begun to giggle with anticipation.

As the 6 o'clock hour approached, she didn't let me out of her sight.

I was frantically searching my mind for the right scenario that "Billy" would describe to my date at the bakery.

Nervously, I dialed the number. I recognized the sweet voice that answered. "Butchar's Bakery, may I help you?"

For a moment I felt guilty for playing a cruel joke on what was obviously a very sweet young lady. There was no turning back now. I attempted to talk a little faster, pretending that I was very agitated, excited, and embarrassed.

"Hello, Meribeth?" I asked. "Yes Billy, are you coming?"

She recognized my voice as the same as the caller of the previous afternoon.

"Well . . . Meribeth . . . I'm . . . only . . . about . . . a . . . block . . . from . . . the . . . bakery . . . but . . . I . . . . had . . . an . . . accident." My niece had moved several feet away from me so that her partially squelched giggles wouldn't reach the telephone.

"Oh, I'm sorry, Billy. Are you all right?"

"I . . . didn't . . . break . . . any . . . bones . . . but . . . I'm . . . all . . . wet."

"What happened?"

"You . . . know . . . it's . . . been . . . raining . . . all . . . day. I . . . took . . . my . . . mom's . . . umbrella . . . and . . . had . . . to . . . steer . . . my . . . bicycle . . . with . . . one . . . hand. A . . . car . . . went . . . through . . . a . . . puddle . . . and . . . splashed . . . me. I . . . veered . . . off . . . the . . . pavement . . . into . . . the . . . mud . . . along . . . the . . . side . . . of . . . the . . . road.

Then . . . I . . . fell . . . in . . . the . . . mud . . . puddle . . . with . . . the . . . bike . . . on . . . top . . . of . . . me. The . . . umbrella . . . is . . . turned . . . inside . . . out . . . and . . . my suit . . . is . . . drenched."

"I'm so sorry, Billy. You'd better get here quick. I'll ask Mr. Butchar if he can loan you some dry clothes."

"No Meribeth, I . . . would . . . be . . . embarrassed. . . . taking . . . you . . . for . . . dinner . . . in . . . a . . . baker's . . . outfit.

Besides . . . the . . . bar . . . between . . . the . . . seat . . . and . . . the . . . handle . . . bar . . . you . . . know. . . . where . . . you . . . were . . . gonna . . . sit . . . is . . . all . . . bent."

My niece had fled and lay on the floor laughing in the adjoining room.

My "date" remained silent and I quickly went on.

"The . . . canopy . . . on . . . my . . . umbrella . . . is . . . sticking . . . straight . . . up . . . and . . . I . . . have . . . to . . . carry . . . my . . . bike. I'll . . . call . . . you . . . another . . . time . . . Meribeth . . . is . . . that . . . all . . . right"?

"Okay, Billy. Be careful now."

"I . . . will . . . Meribeth . . . Bye."

Now, I thought, how was I going to convince my niece Meribeth to talk the real Billy Goad into calling her friend?

I knew I had to try. It only seemed fair.

Besides, who knew? Maybe all this laughter might actually create a romance!

Conundrums and Cabbages

It was in a hotel room in Dallas, Texas, that I made a momentous decision.

Room 3268.

I remember it well.

I had mixed emotions being in Dallas, the city where President. John F. Kennedy had been assassinated the year before. I couldn't really hold that against the city of Dallas. It was Lee Harvey Oswald who had planned to kill the U.S. President. Dallas simply provided him with a place to turn his murderous plan into action when the President visited.

I sat on the edge of that Dallas hotel bed recalling exactly where I'd been when Walter Cronkite of CBS in a "breaking news flash" made the announcement of the assassination. I was in Canada, delivering some background music tapes to one of our Motivating Sound clients in Abbotsford, British Columbia. I turned up the volume on the radio in my green Pontiac. When the somber Cronkite announced with a breaking voice that the President had died, I immediately returned to the U.S. There were no cell phones in the 1960s for me to call home with. I simply raced back and asked the KLYN radio announcer to change the music to classical and instrumental sacred music.

Now, here I was, in the city where that dark page in U.S. history was written.

My prospective client had dropped me off at the hotel. The client was a medium-sized factory representative firm that had expressed an interest in representing the background music and electronic in-store merchandising units made by my company.

I had even written an order for a dozen units. Our manufacturing facilities in Lynden were still very much a "shoestring" operation and I really needed to get back to make sure that the units were properly assembled, tested, packed, and shipped. At the same time there were additional factory rep firms in other parts of the U.S. interested in our products.

There, sitting on that bed in Room 3268, I began to perspire. I felt in crisis.

I was traveling like a madman all over the country writing orders. At the same time, how could I juggle all the balls on my home front?

What about my dear wife and our six children at home?

If this lifestyle kept up, I could become a stranger to them. What was I doing? I asked myself, my head in my hands. Was I alienating myself from my life's greatest blessings, my family?

I made my decision then and there.

Every fiber in my body screamed a resounding "NO!" It was the evening of the following day when I got home. I hugged Margaret and my children. I was at peace with my determination never to exchange my life as a husband and father for the life of a traveling business tycoon. Nothing could ever be of greater value than my family.

I decided I wasn't going to travel as much. I simply had to employ a sales representative that could travel the country. Two weeks later I found a qualified person in Portland, Oregon.

Baron Electronics, Lynden Travel Agency, Motivating Sound, Inc., and KLYN-FM were all businesses in their infancy. They all needed proper nurturing and care. Since I started all those enterprises on a shoestring, I was usually their primary caregiver. Now, though, I realized that I needed help.

I also needed to de-stress.

I could feel a prank being hatched in my mind. That alone reduced the stress I felt.

An announcer named Marvin was my victim. He also had a First Class FCC license. I had given up on my efforts and ability to take adequate time to study for the complicated license.

Since the birth of KLYN-FM broadcast station in November 1960, I not only sold radio advertising, I also had to write the scripts for the client's advertising and type them out in a 30- or 60-second format. Then the client's name was entered into the programming log for the days the ads were scheduled to run.

The announcer on duty was required to pre-read all commercials prior to first time airing. He always had the program log in front of him and all client copy files were in easy reach. This was still before the days when all announcements would be prerecorded and automatically inserted at the correct time in the daily programming schedule.

A grocery store owner had ordered fifteen 30-second announcements. He was also running an ad in the local newspaper that week.

"Just cut my ad out of the paper," he had instructed. "You'll see my low-priced, leader items in the paper. Hammer away at my low prices and make my radio ads sound fantastic."

I sat down behind the old typewriter and, using only one finger, began hitting the keys.

Our radio station studio was located right behind one of the four large front windows of our retail store location. A thermometer located just outside the window was always in view of the announcer while seated behind the studio turntables and microphone.

Marvin, the announcer, looked at the log, then at the large wall-mounted clock in front of him and noticed that the announcement for

ABC Grocery was already four minutes late and the local weather report was also running late.

He grabbed the latest weather report and the ABC Groceries ad copy from the file. Hastily, he pushed the right turntable switch in the "off" position and the microphone control in the "on" position.

Now everyone tuned to 106.5 MHz. could enjoy the deep resonant voice of Marv when he cheerily said into the microphone: "You just heard Harry Belafonte sing 'Danny Boy'.

"We'll continue with more beautiful music on K-Lyn radio after the local weather forecast and an important message from ABC Groceries."

I was in the office adjoining the soundproof studio. I had been monitoring KLYN, which I normally did whenever I wasn't busy with a customer. I was listening to Marvin and, unless he'd caught it in time, I knew what was coming.

I got up from my chair and stood by the double-pane, one-way window, watching Marvin.

I was sure he hadn't pre-read the weather forecast or the ABC Grocery commercial. I smiled to myself with mischievous anticipation.

I saw Marv grab the forecast and nuzzle up close to the microphone. His deep authoritative voice boomed:

"Actually sunny for Whatcom county with shattered scowers devel. . . . ." He paused abruptly. Living in a farming community he knew that the word "scowers" was a word that indicated a serious diarrhea disease among young calves. He vigorously jerked his head, then recovered, "Pardon me. . . . that should be scattered showers developing later in the evening. The current temperature in down town London—" He glanced at the reading on the outside thermometer, then caught himself. "Pardon me, the temperature in downtown Lynden is 68 degrees."

He was clearly annoyed that he hadn't taken the time to pre-read the material. It was too late now, he probably thought. The grocery ad immediately followed the weather forecast.

"Fantastic selection, fantastic service and always fantastic low prices at ABC Groceries at the Fairway Shopping Center in Lynden.

"Just a few of the special prices you'll find in the produce department:

"Bananas, just 29 cents a pound. Locally grown potatoes, ten pounds for just $2.29.

"Garbage only 12 cents a pound."

I was watching him through the small one-way window. He stopped abruptly, jerked his head up briefly, and then looked at his copy again.

"Pardon me, I think that should be cabbage at only 12 cents a pound. For all your produce and grocery needs, shop ABC Groceries at the Fairway Shopping Center in Lynden."

My laughter was like spontaneous combustion. I turned, looked over the office dividing panels and saw Jake at the workbench laughing. He was busy repairing a stereo amplifier and had been monitoring KLYN also. He noticed me looking at him and said, "You got Marv good that time, Sid. I bet he'll never forget to pre-read announcements again prior to broadcast."

"You're right, Jake," I said. I explained how I'd figured out the prank. "I knew he was ignoring the reminders to comply with the clearly posted notice requiring all new copy to be pre-read."

Marvin couldn't hear our exchange in the small soundproof studio. Our monitor indicated that he had just cued up a new record and was playing the tune.

Then the double studio doors flew open. There stood Marv. His face was red as a beet.

He saw both Jake and me laughing.

He glared at me.

"You dirty rat, you made me sound like a bumbling idiot."

I responded, "No, Marv, you sounded more like a polished comedian."

He huffed away in disgust, mumbling, "You won't get by with that stunt again," as he disappeared back in the studio.

I was sure of that.

It's leaking on me

During my 20 years of operating my radio station, then known as KLYN-FM, a variety of mostly young people were employed at various times, gaining experience and exposure to the "romance of radio."

I exposed one of them to the "romance of my gags."

Our studio occupied a small corner of the building, which housed the electronics store, service department, and travel agency. The studio was completely soundproof. A double wall with a small triple-pane window separated it from the station offices. The studio housed the transmitter, audio equipment, and operating console. This console was placed on a custom-made, horseshoe-shaped desk. The operator swivel chair fit precisely between the two turntable-equipped wings of the desk. The microphone was mounted on a flexible gooseneck stand bolted to the desk. When the operator, also known as a disc jockey, needed to read a commercial or weather report, his mouth had to be very close to the microphone, giving him or her no "head wiggle" room. The low false ceiling consisted of attractive corrugated acoustical tile. The entire studio was soundproof.

In addition to employing and training young high school students, we also needed employees with some experience on the team.

Bill was a handsome, tall man with the kind of talent and experience we needed, immaculately dressed with a head adorned with a beautiful layer of thick wavy hair. His real trademark was his impressive deep voice. Perfect for radio. Listeners would no doubt hang on his every word.

One other characteristic soon evident to me was that he had a giant ego. He was clearly impressed with his own voice. Every utterance seemed to say, "Momma, did you hear that?"

It didn't take me long to decide that it was time to test his sense of humor.

With the help of John, another staff member, I hatched an elaborate plot to give Bill a cold shower.

John crawled onto the false ceiling of the studio and punctured a tiny hole through the acoustical ceiling tile. It was totally invisible to anyone inside the studio even if they were studying the ceiling. The hole was positioned precisely above the head of the announcer using the microphone.

No way would he be able to spot the tiny clear plastic hose protruding through the small hole in the ceiling tile!

Now the stage was set and we only needed to wait for evening darkness. The store and radio station office closed at 5 o'clock. The lights would be turned off and only the station operator would be in his chair behind the horseshoe desk in the brightly lit studio.

It was raining hard. At about 7:45 p.m. we entered the completely dark building through the back door with a small flashlight. Of course, I knew that the station log required the operator to read the local weather forecast at 8 p.m.

Numerous listeners far and wide would hear Bill's golden voice booming from their radios to provide them the most recent local weather forecast.

In addition to the small flashlight, we carried a flexible plastic squeeze bottle filled with water. Carefully we navigated through the dark facilities to the station office. The office was dimly lit because the triple pane window separating the studio from the office allowed a degree of illumination. Through this window we were able to observe the announcer behind the microphone without the slightest fear of being detected. Bill glanced at the large wall clock hanging on the studio wall.

He already had the most recent weather forecast in front of him. We were monitoring a small FM-AM radio. As 8 o'clock approached we quickly attached the end of the thin plastic hose to our water-filled squeeze bottle. Our pump was primed.

Bill's booming voice, sounding tinny on our small radio, announced:

"That was the beautiful rendition of 'America the Beautiful' by the inimitable Kenny Rogers. This is KLYN-FM, 106.5 Megahertz on your FM dial. Stay tuned now for the weather forecast."

While Bill played the 15-second music bridge, we were all set to squeeze the daylights out of our bottle, hoping to send the water up through the tiny hose, across the soundproofing material on top of the studio, and onto Bill's head.

We peeked through the small window watching Bill's every move. From our small transistor radio we heard:

"After several days of rain the forecast calls for improving weather, beginning with partial clearing early tomorrow and occasional light showers and sun breaks in the afternoon. The temperatures tomorrow are expected to be in the mid to upper sixties. For tonight the rain is expected to continue unabated and the flood to continue. . . ."

We had been squeezing the bottle for nearly five seconds when it happened. It wasn't just a drip that was descending on poor Bill's beautifully coiffed hair.

It was a small stream.

Bill paused for just a moment, but then proceeded with the weather forecast. To continue talking into the microphone, he needed to be very close. He attempted to avoid the "downpour" by moving his head slightly. It simply cascaded into his ears. In desperation, he pushed his chair back while loudly finishing his weather forecast:

"The flood watch continues to be in effect." He was now five feet away from the microphone when he yelled: "Pardon me, the roof is leaking here. I'm getting soaked."

He quickly hit the turntable start button and stood to shake the water from his hair and suit. He stared up at the ceiling, which had suddenly stopped leaking. We disappeared as quickly and stealthily as we had come. Bill talked about our leaking roof for days but could find no evidence of any leaking anywhere in the building.

He never did learn the source of his baptism.

But I can't help but think that his listeners will always remember that day.

Certainly Bill will never forget and always wonder where that downpour came from.

That cat peed on me

As the various businesses we had spawned increasingly demanded more of my time, I needed to find someone who could run the radio station as well as perform as a sales manager.

A man named Barry accepted that position.

Barry had graduated as music major from college and was eager to provide the KLYN audience with good music and good programming.

Even though my four sons were all growing up in the business, they had not yet attained the level of maturity to assume managerial positions. I hoped I'd be able to hire them as I'd hired Barry, but at times I worried that I was being a bad model for them. Especially when it became apparent that they exhibited a propensity for developing their own pranks!

I remember one very well.

As high school students, it wasn't often that they were home on the weekend. One Friday evening, I was relaxing in my easy chair and paying little attention to Jim and Jerry and their two high school buddies. They were staring through the large window overlooking Front Street. They seemed to be enjoying themselves with much laughter. I assumed they were watching friends hot-rodding at the service station across the street, squealing their tires, and leaving streaks of rubber behind their cars. When I heard sirens and two police cars screeching to a stop in front of our house, I was alarmed. Red lights flashed. I saw the officers heading for the bushy hedge that separated our lawn from the sidewalk. They retrieved a couple of items and headed for our front door, knocking very decisively. My sons and their buddies were no longer laughing. They weren't in front of the window any more either. They knew they'd crossed the line.

The door squeaked as I opened it for the officers.

"Hello, Sid. Are your boys here?" one asked.

"Yes, I think they saw you coming. They ran into the basement."

I noticed the one officer carrying what appeared to human limbs!

I opened the basement door and yelled, "Hey, boys, come on up, will you? You've got company."

Sheepishly they marched up from the cellar, confronting their fates.

"Did you boys hide these under your front yard hedge?" asked one policeman.

"With the feet sticking out over the sidewalk?" asked the other officer.

He pulled out what he had tucked under his arm.

They were two full-size, plastic, inflatable beautiful female legs loosely held together with pantyhose. The pantyhose had undoubtedly been confiscated from their mother's underwear drawer. I recognized the one high-heeled shoe as one of a pair Margaret used to wear.

"You know, guys," the one officer continued, "that's an interesting prank. These things look real, though. People thought a body was lying in the bushes. It nearly caused an accident. We had reports of a murder in front of your house. So, guys, we're just giving you a warning that a prank with the potential to compromise public safety crosses the line. Just a warning this time, but cut it out."

With that he handed me the shapely, air-filled, stocking clad, plastic female legs.

The boys weren't the only ones to get a lesson about the perils of pranksterism.

Should I take the officer's advice and go straight?

Nah!

I'd just be careful that there weren't any accidents involved in my japes.

It was about two weeks later when I remembered that the invisible "rain-maker" hose that had doused Bill the announcer, was still in place. Now that the weather had turned dry and sunny, there might be another application that could startle our radio announcer on duty.

About four in the afternoon, Rick walked into the studio office. He was a bright high school student with a great personality and a bright future. Rick's shift would be from 5:30 to 11:00 p.m. He was a full half hour early.

Suddenly naughty thoughts popped in my head again.

"Rick, I've seen a scrawny yellow cat around here today. I have no idea where the cat came from. I've been trying to catch him, but he's still fast even though he looks sickly. When I tried to catch him in that corner," I said, pointing, "he clambered up and went into hiding in the sound-absorbing material on top of the false studio ceiling. Could you see if you can get him out of there?"

Always cooperative and helpful, Rick immediately headed for the rear of the building to get a stepladder. Just before it was time to start his shift, he reported that he thought he heard some rustling in the loose sound-deadening materials. But he couldn't dislodge the cat from its hiding place.

Marlin and I had agreed to be at the back door of the building about 9:30 that evening.

Rick was the only one in the building and he had no idea that we had sneaked into the dark building too. This time we held our squeeze bottle under the hot water faucet, mixing it with cold to arrive at a comfortable body temperature.

"No, Marlin, don't put the cap on yet."

"Why not?" he asked. "It's nearly full of warm water."

I nodded while taking a small bottle out of my pocket. I had temporarily borrowed that from Margaret's baking supply cabinet. It was yellow food coloring.

Marlin howled with laughter. "I see what we're going to do to poor Rick. What's he going to think?"

"I think we know what he's going to think, don't we, Marlin?"

We attached the end of the plastic tubing to the bottle while Rick placed his mouth close to the desk-mounted microphone, in preparation for announcing the next musical number that he had already selected and cued up a record on one of the two turntables. We laughed with gleeful anticipation knowing that Rick could neither see nor hear us in the soundproof confines of the small studio. Marlin squeezed the bottle as we watched the yellow liquid climb up the clear plastic tube. Up, up and over the edge of the studio ceiling it came. Rick had just started announcing his next choice for entertaining the audience when it happened. Flowing right on top of his head was a tiny stream of liquid.

Startled, he stopped in mid-sentence. In a valiant effort to get away from the waterfall cascading on top of his head, he moved his head as far as the microphone would allow. Now it poured down the side of his head, around his right ear. That's when he realized that this was no ordinary water. It was warm. Without finishing his announcement he hit the start button on the turntable and gave his chair a mighty backward shove as he watched the liquid flow on the desk.

Yes, it was warm . . .

And it was YELLOW!

His startled expression changed to a look of horror and revulsion while he was wiping the right side of his face. We quickly gave the hose a good jerk and gathered the entire length as we made our way to the backdoor exit.

The following day when I walked into the station office, I noticed the stepladder and heard some shuffling on top of the studio ceiling.

"Anybody up there?" I hollered.

"It's me, Sid." I recognized Rick's voice immediately.

"What are you doing, Rick?" I asked.

"I'm looking for that miserable sick cat again, Sid."

"Oh, I'm sure that cat is long gone, Rick," I said. "It might be sick and could have died up there. In that case you maybe able to smell it. Or maybe it has babies op there."

He looked down at me from the edge of the studio ceiling and said, "Well, it's not dead, Sid. That miserable cat peed on me last night."

A Sick Dog and Spiders

Barry, the new general manager of the radio station, wasn't accustomed to the pranks and tricks that at times punctuated our busy lives in the growing organization.

Avoiding becoming a target wasn't an option, though. Barry was well within prankish sights.

In addition to filling the role as manager, Barry also did some on-air announcing shifts. In addition, he had served as sales representative for the station together with my son Jim, who had just returned from college.

Now one day Jim was busily typing away in the office, creating a good-sounding ad for the local farm equipment company. He dutifully entered the name of the client in the station log, which showed the precise time of the actual broadcast of the client's announcement. He knew that Barry would read the first ads live later in the evening. That gave him a naughty idea as he was typing.

Ah, yes!

He was certainly my boy!

The client wanted to make certain that their reputation for outstanding service would be emphasized. As Jim was typing, "We stand behind everything we sell," he added mischievously, "Except our manure spreaders." On the bottom of the page he added: "read copy #2." Now he hoped that Barry wouldn't pre-read the ad prior to airing at

5:25 p.m. If he did, he would pick copy #2 out of the file, the one that didn't contain the "except" line.

At 5:27 p.m. Barry charged red-faced out of the studio. He stomped his foot on the linoleum floor and shook a finger into Jim's face.

"Jim, you stinker, I'd like to put you behind a fully loaded operating manure spreader!"

Laughing, Jim calmly said: "Barry you're supposed to pre-read all scheduled announcements."

Barry was a good and talented man who was troubled by a number of phobias, all of which did nothing to soothe his nervous twitches and rapid eye fluttering. In addition to having a very queasy stomach, even the sight of a small spider sent him into an emotional tailspin.

I couldn't help wondering what effect a *big* spider would have on him.

Jim had studied his "Tricks and Jokes" catalog and found a very real-looking, very large plastic spider covered with some fuzzy body hair.

All that was left to do was place a small screw eye in the ceiling precisely above Barry's desk. Then attach the huge spider to the end of a long hair-like thread and use the screw eye as a thread guide, terminating the long thread through the thin office wall on Jim's desk. We'd have to make sure that the spider was snugly pulled against the screw eye in the ceiling and not easily seen.

All this was accomplished while Barry and I went to the Dutch Treat restaurant for lunch. There was nothing unusual about that. Barry was a frequent and always pleasant lunch partner. This day he was especially hungry, probably because he had skipped breakfast. He ordered a hamburger with soup and French fried potatoes. What happened next I've never been especially proud of. I don't even know why the naughty idea suddenly popped in my head. Why did I feel I needed to test the limitations of Barry's stomach and digestive system? I don't have the answer, but suddenly in the middle of pleasant conversation I put a curious expression on my face and started sniffing. I kept on sniffing, pointing my nose in different directions.

"Hey, Barry, do you smell that?" I said.

"Smell what, Sid?" Barry asked.

"I smell something kind of sour." Immediately Barry put his sniffer in high gear and soon agreed that he, too, discerned an unusual aroma.

Before the food, was served Barry excused himself for a visit to the washroom. When he returned a few minutes, later the food was served and we both proceeded to enjoy our lunch. Casually, I said to Barry, "When you were in the restroom and the waitress brought the food, I asked her about the sour smell."

"What did she say?" Barry asked.

"She said that earlier in the morning there had been a family with two kids and a nice house dog which was sitting on the same chair where you are now sitting. She said that the family dog apparently got sick because it had regurgitated all over the table in that corner." I pointed to where Barry was sitting. Barry's eyes grew wide and in a barely subdued scream he yelled my name dragging out the vowel sound in my name "S I I I D"!

I saw the distress in his face and immediately regretted my cruel joke. That remorse didn't help at all as I watched Barry flee to the men's room at top speed. I had completed my lunch when he returned a full five minutes later, as white as a ghost. He mumbled, "Let's go, Sid."

I quickly left enough money on the table and followed him out of the door to his car. Of course I didn't dare tell him that the whole thing was a fabrication. He might have been in the mood for murder had he known. He dropped me off at the office and went home. Jim was waiting for Barry's return all primed for the descent of the "spider." I was convinced that Barry's phobia about spiders was likely no less intense than the ability of his power of suggestion to wreak havoc on his stomach. Jim wouldn't hear of abandoning the spider idea. It would just have to wait.

The spider is dead

Early one morning, as I walked from our home at 211 Front Street to the radio station at 525 Front Street, I was too preoccupied to notice that it promised to be a beautiful and warm summer day. The smell of fresh-mown grass mingled with blooming flowers along the path. Sprinklers made rainbows in neatly kept yards.

All this beauty was lost on me. It was the second week of August and we were only three days away from the Western Washington District Fair.

This was my busiest week of the year.

In addition to continuing all regular daily business activities, we had to get a booth set up in the commercial building at the fairgrounds and bring in a nice display of organs, pianos, televisions, and stereo systems.

In addition, powerful amplifiers and large speakers needed to be installed at the grandstand show area to provide all the required sound reinforcement for the various scheduled shows during the week. Our broadcast every afternoon live from the fairgrounds had become an annual favorite among many in the station's listening audience. I had been conducting interviews with visitors who attended the fair from many parts of the state of Washington as well as visitors from British Columbia, Canada.

Fortunately, I didn't have to do it alone this week.

Several months earlier I met a young man named Paul at our weekly Toastmaster Club meeting. He impressed me as being a bright, very articulate young man. Just the kind of talent I needed to add a new dimension to our radio-broadcasting schedules. Before long, Paul and I had become good friends. With the two of us debating various topics during our weekly talk program, listeners often got the impression that we were from two different planets. Judging from the "heat" during our debates, many listeners were convinced that the relationship between Paul and me was anything but friendly. They had absolutely no idea that after the program we would peacefully walk along the sidewalk toward the house where my beloved Margaret was waiting for us with coffee and cake. We would visit and laugh about the lively, vigorous disagreements we had staged as we defended our opposing positions.

When I walked into the store, the place was already a beehive of activity. Both our delivery vans were being loaded, the one with speakers, amplifiers and microphones, and the other with organs, pianos, TV sets, handout literature and promotional displays.

Highly responsible employees handled the setup of the commercial booth; our excellent technicians assured that the grandstand sound system and remote radio-broadcast facilities were properly installed and functioning. I would simply stop at the fairgrounds in the evening for a final check.

Jim was sitting at his desk in one of the KLYN offices. Only a thin wall separated his office from Barry's office. Along that wall hung a thin, nearly invisible thread. On the other side of the wall was Barry's desk.

Clinging tightly to the ceiling, right above Barry's desk, was a huge hairy spider.

The spider was held in place with the same thin thread that was fastened securely to a drawer handle on Jim's desk.

"How's it going, Jim?" I asked.

"Hi, dad," Jim responded, "I'm working on a special Fair Week advertising campaign, but mostly I'm just waiting for Barry to get back from lunch."

"Jim, Barry is deathly afraid of spiders, even little ones. He might faint or really go into orbit when he sees that thing."

Jim grinned, "I'm trained in CPR, dad," he said.

"Yes, Jim, but he might kill you after you revive him."

Jim just grinned and said, "I don't think he'll get any more scared than Marilyn did when you rigged a piano wire to her desk drawer."

"Were you there when that happened, Jim?"

"Sure. I was sitting at the other desk in the same office. You had Mark drill a hole through the back panel of the desk, through the thin office divider wall, so you could pull the drawer shut from the TV service bench at least 50 feet away. You could tell when Marilyn opened her desk drawer, because she unwittingly reeled in about a foot of piano wire."

"And do you remember what happened in the office when I closed the drawer with a jerk on the piano wire?"

Jim broke into laughter at the memory.

"Oh, my goodness, dad, Marilyn was preparing the billing for the month. She must have opened the drawer to get something when it slammed shut with a tremendous bang."

"Yes, I remember pulling it harder than I had intended and I heard it slam closed."

"I didn't know it was coming and practically fell off my office chair."

"And Marilyn?"

Jim laughed again. "Oh, wow, she actually fell over with her office chair on top of her. I quickly helped her get upright again."

"Did you tell her how that happened?"

"No, she had no idea how that drawer slammed shut all by itself."

"Did you tell her then, Jim?" I asked.

"Are you kidding? She would have bit my ear off and gone after you for some painful revenge."

"Yah, I'm glad she didn't find out until many years later."

Jim, still laughing, said, "Actually, I think brother Ger told her when she started working for him years later."

I heard the outside office door open and quickly whispered, "Here comes Barry, Jim."

I seated myself behind my desk, which was located very close to Barry's desk.

We were obviously very busy.

Barry seemed quite cheery when he said, "Hi Sid. Hi, Jim, I sold a couple of good Fair Week radio-advertising packages this morning."

"Wonderful, Barry," I said. I was working on scheduling Fair Week manpower, listing myself as being at our triple-duty activities from 10 a.m. to 11 p.m. daily.

"Hey, Barry, you'll be able to work the studio switchboard during the daily remote broadcast from the fair, won't you?"

I noticed in my peripheral vision that the huge spider had just commenced its slow descent.

Without looking up, Barry responded, "Sure, no problem, Sid. We'll do it just like last year."

He was concentrating on entering the advertising schedules into the station log for broadcast during Fair Week. From the corner of my eyes I noticed that Jim was reeling out the thin thread very slowly, which made the hairy soft rubber spider's descent look very realistic. It certainly looked like a real, very much alive, huge spider, complete with little pinhead beady eyes.

I was startled when suddenly I heard the most fearsome primal scream I'd ever heard. Barry raced past my desk, screaming as he headed for the exit. Before disappearing he cried, "Sid, kill that thing!"

I yelled, "What thing?" but he was heading down the alley to the safety of his car.

About an hour later he called. "Sid, did you get that big spider?"

"Wow, that was a big one, Barry," I responded.

"Did you kill it, Sid?"

"I gave it a mighty whack with the big fly swatter. It went sailing across the room and landed under Jim's desk."

"Sid, is it dead?" Barry asked impatiently with fear still in his voice.

"I stepped on it. You can bet it's not alive."

Something that was alive, though, was the sound of laughter ringing in the room when I hung up.

On the Bus to the Fair

It was Monday morning, the first day of the annual western Washington Fair in Lynden. Our electronic merchandise display was in place. The remote broadcast booth had been tested and retested, as well as the grandstand sound amplification system.

Now I was sitting in the shuttle bus, which weaved its way through Lynden, picking up fairgoers at various designated pick-up areas. With one hand I steadied my briefcase, which was loaded with wireless microphone equipment, while with the other hand I was scribbling notes about items "not to be forgotten." Then I looked out of the window and tried to relax, wondering if Paul Elvig had already arrived at the fairgrounds.

Sitting on that bus, thinking about Paul, I remembered a funny story about Paul's father.

Paul and I were both members of the local Toastmaster Cub.

Every week at Toastmasters, members of the club got the chance to practice their public speaking. Paul's father Ken was also a member.

Paul's Dad was the first that week to speak. Toastmasters speak for three long minutes, totally extemporaneous without prior preparation. Their speeches were always based on a topic scribbled by another member from a "table topic group." Participating speakers were not given an opportunity to look at the topic on the paper until they stood to speak.

Mr. Elvig took a quick glance at the topic as he unfolded it.

It simply contained a three-letter word: "Sex." He calmly read it out loud, refolded the scrap of paper, placed it on the table in front of him and, making eye contact with the audience, began.

"Gentlemen."

There were no female Toastmaster members at that time.

With skill and dignity, he articulated how sexual activity is the only means for any and all species inhabiting the planet earth, including humans, to assure that life on the planet continues from one generation of species to the next.

I didn't hear until later about what happened when Mr. Elvig got home that evening.

Mr. Elvig's wife always asked him if he had to speak at the meeting that evening. Then they would discuss his topic together. Tonight's topic was not one he wanted to discuss with his wife. When he arrived home he quickly sat in his rocking chair and scooped up the paper, hiding his head completely behind it.

"Did you have to speak tonight, Ken?" his wife asked. In a barely audible voice, he grunted "Uh huh," hoping that his wife would not ask any follow-up questions.

"What subject did you have to speak about, Ken?"

Oh, golly, here it was. Just what he had feared.

He cleared his throat and mumbled feebly, "Sailing."

Then he continued pretending to be in deep concentration on what he was reading in the paper. Fortunately his wife dropped the subject.

Now, I knew nothing about this conversation when I saw Mrs. Elvig in town the following day.

I greeted her warmly. "I chatted with your husband at Toastmasters last night."

She looked at me with serious curiosity. "How did Ken do on his speech last night?"

Her question took me completely off guard. Sex is not generally a subject I discuss with female acquaintances. I scratched my head vigorously, pretending to neutralize a serious itch, and said, "Ken always does a great job with any subject he's asked to speak on. Last night was no different. He knew what he was talking about."

She looked at me somewhat disbelieving and as she turned to continue walking along the sidewalk.

She said, "I can't imagine him knowing much about last night's subject. He only did it twice, the first time he got a headache, and the second time his hat blew off."

The bus stopped numerous times on the way to the fairgrounds as I thought about that story, smiling.

I was relaxed and giggled inwardly as I recalled my trip with Paul Elvig to our nation's capitol, where we were going to attend a broadcasting convention and visit with some of our Washington State elected officials.

The trip was during the early 1970s, when air travel was both pleasant and luxurious—especially when seated in the upstairs lounge aboard a huge Boeing 747. The air was smooth, without even a trace of turbulence. Paul was peacefully smoking a cigar while we engaged in pleasant conversation. He had his arm draped around the adjoining seat, which together with his seat, was located along the exterior wall of the airplane. Suddenly he looked alarmed and jumped up. He bent over the adjoining seat and attempted to move the back of the seat forward allowing him to look behind the seat.

"What's the matter Paul?" I said to satisfy my own curiosity.

"I dropped my cigar behind the seat," he responded. "I see it lying on the carpet, but I can't reach it."

"Let me take a look, Paul. My arms are skinnier."

He made room for me and I saw the smoking cigar. I stretched out on my stomach in front of the seat and tried to reach it. I said to Paul, "My arms are skinny enough but they're too short."

Just then a stewardess emerged from the galley and quickly took in the scene. Here was one guy lying on the floor, and the other trying to drape his body over a seat. Somewhat alarmed she exclaimed, "What's going on, gentlemen?"

Paul explained that his cigar had fallen on the floor behind the seat and seemed to be out of reach.

The stewardess looked quickly and noticed that not only was the cigar smoking, but the carpet behind the seat had started smoldering. Quickly she disappeared in the galley and equally quickly reappeared with a long fork. Now she got down on hands and knees trying to bring the lit cigar within reach.

All to no avail.

The carpet was really smoldering now and the stewardess became alarmed. She scrambled to her feet and said, "This doesn't look good, gentlemen. I have to get the captain."

With that, she headed rapidly for the cockpit.

Within seconds she reappeared, heading for where we were standing with the captain in tow. He removed his captain's hat so that he could get a closer look at the problem behind our seat. It wasn't necessary. A small cloud of smoke was rising from behind our seat and other passengers began converging onto the scene. The captain didn't even take the time to put his cap back onto his balding head. He just dropped it on the seat and exclaimed, "Jeez, Oy! Oy!", then raced back to the cockpit. He grabbed a fire extinguisher and quickly doused the smoldering cigar and carpet with a thick layer of white foam.

It was late in the evening when we finally checked into the Washington, D.C. Hilton. The convention hotel. Paul was the first to arrive at the check-in desk, where an attractive young lady, with a genuine smile on her face, welcomed him.

I was right behind him. The attractive agent smiled at him expectantly when he said, "My name is Paul Elvig. We're booked into two adjoining rooms."

Halfway turning toward me, he continued, "I'm accompanied by my friend. Please meet Senator Dexter Gaspasser."

I was embarrassed to tears, but the cute clerk and Paul were both laughing hysterically.

Fun at the Fair

The bus I'd been on, daydreaming, reached its destination and growled to a halt near the main gate of the fairgrounds.

The ferris wheel spun slowly over the bustling scene. Piping carousel music filled the air, alongside with the merry smells of popcorn and cotton candy.

I gathered my cables, connecters, headphones and microphones. I flashed my press pass at the admissions booth. Then I hurried to a remote broadcast booth. I spotted Paul while wandering somewhat aimlessly among the exhibits in the commercial building.

I guess he'd been waiting for me.

Quickly I grabbed a box of microphone cables that were needed in the grandstand area. I walked up to him from behind and greeted him. "Hi, Paul," I called. "I need to bring these cables to the grandstand. Why don't you walk along? Maybe we can plan our agenda for this afternoon's remote broadcasts."

He quickly picked up the pace. "Good thinking, Sid," he responded. "I've got some ideas I want to run by you."

"Just don't you call me Senator Dexter Gasspasser on the air, like you did in D.C., Paul."

He slapped himself on the knee as we were walking, at the same time laughing his head off.

I didn't laugh at all as I thought of my blushing face in that Washington D.C. lobby. I consoled myself with the thought that there would be opportunities where revenge would surely be mine. Almost instantly an idea for vengeance hit me. We were walking briskly along on our way to the grandstand area. The pedestrian traffic was not too heavy and only occasionally did we pass people that were walking slower than our pace. Paul was on my right.

We were practically marching in step and had just passed a couple of women when I decided it was time to strike.

Without breaking stride, I lifted my right leg and landed a swift kick with the side of my foot on Paul's well-padded posterior.

He couldn't tell that I was the culprit!

I'd finessed the move with the grace of Fred Astaire punting in a Super Bowl.

Paul stopped in his tracks.

He swiveled to face the two women immediately behind us. He glared at the beefier one of the two, shook his pointer finger and loudly exclaimed, "You kicked me."

Seeing Paul's angry mug, they vigorously shook their heads with fervent denial. Both pointed at me, almost yelling, "No, no, he did it."

I had already removed the innocent look from my face and merely grinned when Paul, still not willing to believe that I, walking so nicely by his side, never breaking stride, could have delivered such a blow to his posterior.

I quickly said, "That's how Senator Gasspasser treats his best friends."

We both laughed again.

During our return from the grandstand area, Paul turned on his tape recorder. We would prerecord some segments of our daily broadcast. Paul described the scene and overall activity at the fairgrounds this beautiful Saturday afternoon, amidst the whirs and shrieks of the roller coaster and the happy rumbles of the crowds. Frequently, he would turn the microphone to me for a response to comments he had just made. We would stop to chat with someone whenever we saw a noteworthy fairgoer. However, most of our interviews were broadcast live and were not prerecorded.

Now this was in the late 1970s. Wireless microphone technology was in its infancy. We did use wireless microphones, but the range was limited to approximately 200 feet.

Where we stood now was still too far from our broadcast booth in the commercial building. Paul switched the cassette to the "record" position as a couple of young boys were approaching. I judged them to be about ten or twelve years of age. We had never before interviewed children from the fair. I suspect that Paul had a sudden inspiration to pretend to be Art Linkletter for a while. Mr. Linkletter had long aired a television show called "Kids say the darndest things."

"Hi, boys, my name is Paul Elvig. We're talking to different people at the fair for broadcast over KLYN radio. What's your first name?"

"My name is Johnny and my friend is Pete," the older of the two boys responded.

"Is that your favorite fair snack?" Paul asked, as he pointed to the two cotton candy cones the boys were busy devouring. "We like snow cones too," said Johnny, "but it's a little cold today. Pete and me are planning to each buy a sausage on a stick a little later".

"What do you kids enjoy the most at the fair?"

Pete was quick to respond, "First, the rides, and then the horses and the cows. Man, they're such big animals and you don't have to be scared of them at all."

"You guys must not live on a farm," said Paul.

Almost in unison they replied, "We live in Vancouver and we come here every year with Pete's mom and dad."

Paul nodded his head and asked if they were coming back the next day. Even before Paul had completed the question they were both shaking their heads and explaining that it was the last day of the fair.

Tomorrow they would have to go to Sunday school in Vancouver. Placing the microphone close to the youngest boy's mouth he asked, "Do you like Sunday school, Pete?"

The boy shook his head, which required that Paul had to explain for the listening audience that the boy's answer was "no." Then Pete started talking and said, "Sometimes I like it."

"What don't you like about it, Pete?"

"When the teacher asks questions that I can't answer. But last week she asked me a question and I knew the answer."

"What question did she ask, Pete?"

"She asked if I thought Noah fished every day for food when he was on the ship for forty days. And I knew the answer."

"What was your answer Pete?"

"I said Noah couldn't have fished a lot 'cause he only had two worms."

Now Johnny quickly chimed in: "Teacher asked me if I knew why Lot's wife turned into a pillar of salt when she looked back."

"Did you know the answer, Johnny?" asked Paul.

"No," Johnny said. "I didn't know the answer, but I told her that my mom looked back once and she turned into a telephone pole."

We both laughed and Paul must have really felt like Art Linkletter, who had demonstrated on his television program for many years that kids would indeed say "the darndest things."

Fair Pranks?

Our remote live broadcasts from the fairgrounds usually started about three in the afternoon.

Paul would usually arrive shortly after one o'clock. That gave us time to pre-plan our actual broadcast time. Often we would prerecord certain segments just in case we needed some filler material.

One day, with a mischievous glint in his eyes, Paul told me he had a plan, one that was well within our prankish traditions. Paul had prepared an elaborate prop for us to use on a waitress at a food booth. He kept the curtain veiled over the nature of this prop, but did explain that the food concession he had targeted was outside the range of our wireless microphone.

Could we use our recorder to tape the result of the practical joke for our show?

I quickly slipped fresh batteries in the portable cassette recorder and we headed out onto the fairgrounds.

It was a lovely summer day. The sun peeked out from scuds of cumulus clouds piled like white cotton candy in the sky. The smell of fried onions hung in the air. The amusement park rides turned and spun like the interior of some fairy's clock.

Paul grinned slyly as we marched toward the area where most food concessions were located. Many of the booths were operated by local groups to raise funds for their organizations or other charities. Most if not all of the workers were volunteers not necessarily experienced in food preparation and service.

"Let's go to that one," Paul said. He pointed to a booth with a large banner advertising hamburgers with French fries for 79 cents. The squared U-shaped bench surrounding the counter was tightly occupied with hungry fairgoers enjoying the juicy hamburgers.

"Paul, there's no place to sit right now. Why don't we take a look in the cow barn and come back a little later?"

Paul agreed and we walked to the farm buildings.

We passed through large double barn doors where dozens of beautiful large Holstein milk cows were contentedly munching the green alfalfa hay while others were comfortably bedded down on the floor of their stalls and chewing their cuds.

"Have you ever tried to milk a cow, Paul?" I asked.

"No" he said, "but that can't be too hard."

"Say, why don't you try it and I'll record your hand-milking efforts. Maybe we can have a little contest and you describe my own feeble efforts after you're done."

He handed me the recorder and microphone while he sat on his heels and placed his right hand firmly around a fleshy handle from which the milk would soon flow.

I switched the tape recorder on.

Paul wore an intense, determined expression on his face as his fist tightened and loosened alternately around the cow's milk handle.

Nothing came out.

Not a drop.

More determined now, he shifted his position and decided to try his left hand. He selected what I'm sure he hoped would be a more milk-filled udder.

With a defeated look now he turned to me.

"Sid, it's just early afternoon. I think the cows don't have any milk in their tanks or they just don't let it down into their teats. I can't get a drop out of this dumb cow. You try it, Sid. Good luck." With that he got to his feet and reached for the recorder that held the testimony of his defeat and surrender.

I got down on my haunches beside the cow.

Familiar territory!

The smell of straw and cow dung tripped my milking mechanism. I gently placed my hand around the "handle" while massaging the area just above it with thumb and forefinger to make sure I'd collect a healthy squirt of milk ready for release.

A surprise release.

Inwardly I snickered. Paul had no idea that I had learned the skill of hand milking cows when I was only seven years old, growing up on a small farm in the northern part of Holland. He had no idea that, in addition to starting in business, I had continued farming into the early sixties. He had no idea that I was a master marksman with milk. Even when it came to placing a powerful squirt of milk right into the face of one of my barn cats at a distance of fifteen feet!

We were beginning to attract an audience.

Perhaps it was the official looking KLYN-FM press badge Paul was wearing while he was busy talking into the microphone describing what he thought were my feeble efforts to make a drop of milk appear. No wonder. I'd put a defeated expression on my face all the while I was loading my "milk cannon."

Paul had briefly turned off his recorder and explained to the person nearest to him that I was trying to get some milk out of that cow. The middle aged, farmer-type man looked at me. He immediately saw by the way I was holding the "handle" that I was no stranger to hand milking a cow. I heard him say to Paul, "That guy is priming the pump."

Fortunately, Paul didn't know what that meant, but I knew I didn't have any time to waste. I looked at Paul with a silly look on my face to deflect the truth of my real intent. I was simply measuring the direction and distance to my target.

I didn't want him to notice that I was curving the loaded little "cannon" in his direction.

Just as he smiled sympathetically and condescendingly while at the same time beginning to talk into the microphone again, there was a powerful "PZZZZTT."

A solid, powerful squirt of milk splashed right into the middle of his round face. His reaction could not have been more startled, had he been struck by lightening.

Lightning would have been more understandable.

To get stung in the face with a "milk gun" totally defied all comprehension.

It later took me several minutes to edit from the tape what he said. There were some choice words Paul had uttered after he got shot by some of the contents of a cow udder.

The Flying Patty

The pranks at the fair did not end with the cow.

It took a while before Paul cleaned that milk I'd squirted from his face. It took even longer for him to regain his composure. He had already exhausted all the uncomplimentary names he could call me. Some of the people standing around looked aghast, while others grinned. The middle-aged farmer roared with laughter, yelling, "Good shot, man. Good shot."

Paul was still wiping his face when I whispered, "You didn't know Senator Gaspasser was such a good shot, did you, Paul?"

Smiling, he promised revenge.

By the time we were finally on the way to the food booth with stomachs growling in anticipation of the arrival of a juicy hamburger complete with fries, Paul had calmed down.

"I had no idea you knew how to milk a cow any better than I did. Where did you learn that?"

"I learned hand milking cows when I was only seven years old, Paul. I was born and raised on a small farm in the small town of Opende, right on the border between the two northernmost provinces of Groningen and Friesland in the Netherlands."

"Here I thought you were always a city boy, Sid."

"You know Paul, I moved off my forty-acre farm only a few years ago. That's when I sold my eighteen cows, and to help close the deal, I threw in my two milk stools free with the sale of the cows."

Paul looked at me very skeptically. "Now, Sid, you started the broadcast station in 1960. That'll be ten years ago this year. In addition you had already started your electronics business many years earlier. Plus you added a travel agency, a Western Union office, background music services and who knows what else. There's no way you could have juggled all those business balls *and* milked eighteen cows *and* run a forty-acre farm. No way!"

"Paul," I said, "I never saw that as a problem nor as an unusual achievement. I came home from my business, quickly pulled a coverall over my shirt-and-tie business attire and headed for the barn. I used three DeLaval milking machines. Except, occasionally I'd nearly squirt the eyes out of my barn cat with a powerful streak of milk."

"By golly Sid, I believe it. That streak of milk did sting my face."

"I'm sorry, Paul, I should have warned you first," I said with a disingenuous look on my face.

"Did you have time to eat, Sid, or pay attention to your kids?" Paul asked.

"Margaret would quickly feed me supper. I'd hold the smaller kids on my lap for a while. Then I'd often have to make evening service calls to repair some customer's TV sets." He looked at me as though he wasn't sure he could believe me.

"Man, you certainly were burning the candles at both ends."

"I couldn't do it any more, Paul. My energy level is fading lately. I really never knew what it would be like to be tired. Now I do get tired and wonder what 'disease' I'm getting. I shouldn't be feeling the effects of advancing age yet."

Paul didn't respond. He was focusing on the food booth he had targeted earlier.

"I could sure go for a bite to eat," said Paul. "Hey, look there are a few empty places on the bench along the front of the counter." We quickly claimed the space and settled down for some nourishment.

Paul placed the still milk-stained tape recorder on the seat beside him. "Milking is hard work Paul," I said. "I'm sure hungry," he responded.

Hamburgers, French fries, and milkshakes were the specialty of this booth. It was already past one in the afternoon. We were hungry. After ordering, Paul reached into his pocket and revealed a regular carpenter nail. Right in the center of the nail he had knotted the end of a thin grey sewing thread. It looked as though the loosely rolled up thread was at least 50 feet long.

"What are you going to do with that, Paul?" I asked. He grinned slyly again and said, "Just wait and see. I'm not sure it's going to work, but I'm going to give it a try."

He laid the microphone on the counter where he could quickly reach the switch to place it in the "on" position. I had no idea what he had up his sleeve; I suspected that he was planning to play a trick on one of the hard-working volunteer waitresses of the concession. They were very busy running back and forth from the counter to the back, where two guys were busy flipping hamburger patties.

A friendly lady of about forty took our order. We each ordered a hamburger with fries and a milkshake. Paul busied himself with his "nail-on-a-string." He carefully unwound the thread and let it gather on the ground under the outside of the service counter. He clearly wanted the thread available for rapid unwinding without offering resistance or getting hung up on something.

Within minutes our order was delivered. With growing curiosity I watched Paul remove his hamburger from the little waxed-paper bag. He threaded or "stitched" the nail right through the center of the beef patty and replaced the bun while sliding it back into the paper bag. The thin black thread, now hanging out of the hamburger baggy, surely wouldn't be visible to harried, hurried, super-busy volunteer staff.

That's when it happened.

"Ma'am, ma'am," Paul called to get the waitress's attention. When she turned to look he motioned for her to come. "Ma'am, could you take this hamburger and add a good slice of cheese?"

"Oh, you wanted a cheeseburger," said the waitress.

"Yes, please, can you still do that?"

"Oh sure." With a flourish, she whisked his paper hamburger bag and quickly headed for the kitchen area. She didn't notice the nearly invisible gray thread unreeling rapidly through Paul's hand until she was approximately twenty feet away from where Paul and I were sitting at the counter.

I quickly glanced at Paul, not having a clue about his intentions. Clearly he was in the middle of an elaborate trick. The intense expression on his face indicated that he wasn't at all confident that it would work out as he planned. Suddenly he raised his hand and gave it a mighty jerk. The result was immediate and most startling. The hamburger patty swiftly departed from between the two half buns and smacked into Paul's face.

To say that the waitress was shocked would be an understatement. In an instant she saw that the hamburger patty she was carrying had suddenly departed the bag and impacted the face of the customer with such force as to nearly drive his nose into his face.

She threw up her hands and the hamburger patty-less bag with bun and French fries went flying. All the while the poor "customer" was yelling: "Hey, you threw a hamburger in my face."

The hapless waitress's eyes went wide and mouth opened. She took one look at the poor customer's messy face and started crying loudly while quickly fleeing out of sight.

An apologetic headwaiter approached Paul, who was now laughing hysterically, waving off the apologies as he said, "She didn't do anything wrong. I just pulled a nasty trick on her." All the while still wiping his face, he went on, laughing: "Please tell her that I'm sorry, that I'll pay for the hamburger I messed up. I'll pay for a new one and will leave her a good tip."

As we strode back through the swirl of lights and laughter, and the smell of grease and popcorn that was the fair, I mused.

It had certainly been an eventful day at the fair with Paul Elvig.

Fighting Fear

I gazed through the one-way window in my office, looking out onto the retail floor of the store.

I saw the man approaching.

I felt a sense of foreboding.

"Rook" Van Halm was not only our company bookkeeper; he was a business partner and a good friend. Rook was a tall, handsome man with earnest, deep brown eyes and thinning black hair. His real first name was Wigger. It was his black hair which caused his father to give him the nickname when he was born at their home in Amsterdam. His new baby son had reminded the father of the big black-feathered bird known as a rook. That nickname would stick for the rest of his life. Most people never knew that his real name was Wigger.

Even watching him approach my office, I could tell that something was seriously wrong. He carried an envelope in his hand. He stopped and just looked at me without saying a word. But the expression on his face couldn't hide his anxiety, concern and almost deep desperation. I knew whatever information the letter he was holding conveyed could not be good.

"Sid, this may be the last straw," he said.

With that he opened the letter and started reading.

"Musilec Services, Ltd., from Vancouver, B.C. has declared bankruptcy. All payments to vendors have been indefinitely suspended and all merchandise in the company's warehouse and facilities is being held subject to the final disposition of the Bankruptcy Court."

The color must have drained from my face.

"Rook," I said, "they owe us thousands of dollars. They are our largest distributor to clients of our background music machines."

Staring at me with great concern in his eyes, Rook said, "They were running about thirty to sixty days late in paying their invoices. That's why I have many invoices I haven't been able to pay for lack of money. Now it's hopeless, Sid. We can't survive this."

For what seemed like minutes, we just looked at each other. I knew I was scheduled to go with my son Alan to Seattle to pick up a van load of store retail merchandise. I was the owner of a company which now might face bankruptcy also. I could see the same thoughts were going through Rook's mind as he looked at me with despair. The economic well being of his family hinged largely upon the economic well being of the company of which he was a partner and employee. I couldn't leave him for the day in a state of total despair.

"Rook, during the past year it seems we've received a number of miracles of survival. Maybe it's because we asked God to show us the way that the miracles occurred. We need a big one now, Rook. Let's not give up on our faith."

For a moment he stared at the floor and dabbed at his eyes. Then, in the presence of no one except the Almighty, we embraced each other. It was a confirmation of our common faith in God and our faith in the future of our company in spite of a hopeless seeming present. I quickly hurried out the front door where Alan had been waiting impatiently.

There was little conversation. Alan was the youngest of my four sons. I certainly couldn't reveal the depths of my despair and the multitude of negative thoughts that ricocheted through my brains. Alan didn't need to know yet about the fever of business life and what it was like to look failure squarely in the face. I needed to kick myself out of the pit of negative thinking.

As we were entering Skagit County, Alan began fiddling with the CB radio he had installed in our Ford van. CB radio was a new and exciting way for truckers to talk to the fellow big rig drivers who spent many hours of their days piloting eighteen to thirty wheelers across the highways of America. The transmission and reception range of CB radios was limited to a few miles. But it was sufficient for many truckers to chat and at times warn fellow truckers that "Smokey" was up ahead with a radar speed trap. Besides, it served to reduce boredom during the many hours behind the wheel. Alan was listening to the conversation between two truckers who were traveling along I-5 about three miles apart. I started listening to the conversation and noticed it had nothing to do with their profession as truckers. They called each other by their first name and obviously knew each other's families.

"What's ye laughin' about, Ben?"

"Oh, I was just thinking about really foolin' my wife Stella last Saturday night."

The sentences snarled through the speakers like electric ghosts.

There was quite a bit of static at times. I had to concentrate to get the conversation between the two truckers.

"Well, Chuck, I went out with some buddies last Saturday night and you know Stella goes ballistic if I don't get home by midnight."

"Okay, Ben, I hear ye. You got in late and you're in the doghouse."

"No, no, Chuck. I fooled her."

"How 'd ye do that?" asked Ben.

"Well, you know, Ben, we have this cuckoo clock that Stella hears most hours of the night. When I stumbled into the living room on my way to the bedroom, the old bird cuckooed four times. I just knew Stella would hear it. Holy smokes, it was four in the morning, Ben. I stopped dead in my tracks and cursed. Then I got a bright idea and did a near perfect imitation of the old clock by cuckooing eight more times. Then I stumbled into bed."

"Did she notice?" asked Chuck,

"She stirred but didn't say anything."

"Oh, man, you were lucky," said Ben.

"That's what I found out the next morning," Chuck responded.

"What happened the next morning," Ben wanted to know.

"Oh, man, you wouldn't believe it. We sat down for breakfast. We usually don't talk much. Stella asked, "How are you this morning, Charlie-boy?" I was somewhat surprised by her pleasant tone of voice. I mumbled, "I'm fine. How are you, Stella?"

"'Well, Chuck, I'm fine, but there's something haywire with our cuckoo clock.' I said, 'How's that, Stella?' 'Well, last night it cuckooed four times, then it cursed two times, then it cuckooed eight more times.'"

We laughed as hard as Ben and Chuck.

We were entering Seattle now and Alan turned off the CB radio. I felt much better. God was looking after me, I realized later. A big laugh was just what I needed.

My Bessie is Sick

We went to Zerega Distributing Company and loaded our van with an assortment of Motorola TV sets and a few console stereos. The van was pretty much full. They handed me the invoice. It would be due in 30 days. We had an excellent credit reputation and the company knew the invoice would be paid. The butterflies started churning my stomach.

Only I knew that our company was on the verge of bankruptcy. Our largest background music equipment distributor had left us with thousands of dollars in uncollectible receivables. Unsuccessfully I attempted to ban the hopelessness of our financial condition from my mind.

Facing the failure of a business one has started is enormously stressful. Margaret had just given birth to our sixth child, Julie. Not only was the economic security of my family at stake, the economic well being of my employees also weighed heavily. The more I consciously struggled with impending business disaster, the more inevitable it seemed and the stress level rose.

I had experienced in the past that my subconscious was often better at developing solutions to seemingly unsolvable difficulties. But as long as my conscious being was nervously searching for the possibility of a solution, my subconscious was paralyzed. I needed to unwind and utilize the relaxing powers of laughter. Creative humor always works.

We were northbound now on our return trip to Lynden.

"Hey, Alan, that was fun listening to the CB radio," I said.

Promptly he hit the on-off switch and instantly the static sound of CB radio filled the cabin of our van. "Can I try to talk to someone on the CB radio, Alan?"

He eyed me somewhat suspiciously; probably knowing that dad could easily do something embarrassing and crazy. "You know, dad, you need to be careful because those guys in the big trucks are usually not too far away and they could easily spot you. You don't want to get squeezed off the road by a big, angry trucker pushing an eighteen wheeler."

"Don't worry, Alan. I used to be an amateur radio operator before I started KLYN-FM."

"Oh sure, I remember, dad," Alan responded, "I still remember your call sign: W7VFN."

"Hey, good memory, Al."

"Thanks, dad, but I also remember that some of your ham radio buddies thought that the VFN call letters stood for Very Funny Nut."

I grinned. He was right again. "Alan," I asked, "with my amateur radio station, if I wanted to talk to someone I'd just say, CQ, CQ, CQ. This is W7VFN calling CQ on this frequency."

Alan nodded.

"How do they try to raise someone on CB, Alan?"

He began to explain when I decided to push the Transmit button on the CB and in a shaky, accented "old man" voice, I said, "Anybody out there dat cud help me out?"

I didn't have to wait long for an answer. "Hey, old buddy, what can I do for ye?"

Now I had to think of something fast before I responded and pushed the transmit button again. "Oh, say, tanks. I haff only wun cow. It took sick on me. Now I haff it in de horse trailer behind me pick-up. And I's look'n for a cow hospital."

Alan almost choked on the bite he was taking from his apple. I could almost hear the grin in the trucker's voice when he answered, "Okay, buddy, you need a vet."

Quickly I pushed the button again and said, "A fat? What's a fat?"

Equally quickly he responded, "A vet is a veterinarian and there are cow doctors. Where are you, old buddy?"

I had expected that question and needed to be careful. I knew the trucker would be looking for an old pick-up with a cow-carrying horse trailer in tow. He would be looking for an old farmer driving it. He would never think that this crazy old man was riding in a maroon van emblazoned with Baron Electronics along both sides.

I ignored his question and said, "I saw a hospital sign a ways back and pulled in. I walked through the big glass door. There wuz a fellow sitt'n behind a counter in a white suit wit' a dingemajig hangen around his neck. I was in my overall an' boots. Everyt'ing was so clean. No trace of cow manure anyplace. I asked the feller in de white suit, 'You got any buddy here who can look at me Bessie?'"

"Is that your wife?" he said.

"No, man, thas me sick cow out in de horse trailer. De man just laugh at me and says that me wuz in de wrung place."

Alan couldn't laugh out loud, but he was shaking and had trouble staying in his lane. When my CB buddy answered, after what seemed like a long time of silence, I could still hear him laugh. "My goodness, buddy you've got problems. Where are you now?" he asked again.

"I juz seen a sign det says Everett," I responded.

"Okay," he said, just turn off the freeway in Everett on Pacific Avenue. Stop some place and ask somebody for directions to an animal hospital. Good luck, old buddy."

"T-t-tank you," I muttered.

We did take the right lane exit off I-5 and turned left onto Pacific Avenue. Actually it was long past lunchtime and we decided to take in a little nourishment. We soon were seated in a booth at Denny's, which was conveniently located right along Pacific Avenue.

Alan looked at me and laughed again. "You're crazy, dad," he said.

"No, Alan, I'm just working hard at trying to keep from going really crazy."

"Well, dad, I think you're getting close." He didn't have any idea that I was virtually in mortal combat with the pressures of business that threatened to overwhelm me. I didn't want to burden him with my problems. He was young yet and it was likely that he would also learn that the journey of a human life is not always along a flowery path of ease.

"You know, Alan, laughter is powerful medicine against depression, emotional, and mental stress, as well as all types of diseases. Just imagine, this trucker is probably telling the story to numerous other truckers via their CB radios. He may do that for several days. My goodness, Al, maybe dozens of truckers are going to feel better because of poor old Bessie and because I'm a little crazy."

We were soon heading North again on I-5. My hand fingered the invoices in my pocket and instantly fear grabbed me with a paralyzing intensity. Me? Going bankrupt? Completely failing my wife and family? They depended on me to be a reliable provider. They depended on my judgments and skills as a businessman. I wouldn't be able to live with myself. Oh, God, I needed help.

I pushed the CB switch to the "ON" position. I knew that the trucker we had talked to earlier was long out of CB reception area. Before Alan knew what was happening, I was talking again. "Hello, hello, hello," I almost yelled. With a voice that sounded fearful and hysterical I continued, "Can anybody help me?"

Almost immediately a voice responded: "What's the problem, old buddy?"

"Me jus turned off the highway and me whole trailer tip over goin' 'round de corner. And Bessie's in it. Where are you?"

Now the trucker had alarm in his voice. "Oh, goodness sakes. I'm almost in Bellingham. You tipped your whole trailer over and there was a woman in it? Where are you?"

"Jus' off de highway north of Mount Vernon."

"Oh, goodness sakes, I can't turn my big rig around, but I can call the State Patrol for you. How come you had a woman in the trailer?"

"No, no, Bessie no woman. Bessie, she is me cow. Bessie sick and me jus' get back from the cow hospital in Everett. I was gonna stop and milk me Bessie cause me always milk Bessie dis time of day. And me family needs de milk."

I could tell the trucker was laughing now when he pushed his transmit button again. "Oh, fellow, this is crazy. You're pulling my leg. What kind of rig are you driving?" he asked.

"It's old Ford pickup truck wit me horse trailer and Bessie in it behind. Me horse trailer unhitched and lay on de side and Bessie kickin' like a steer and me milk pail is flat like a pancake. Oh, man I need help to get the whole caboodle right side up again."

With his right hand on the steering wheel, Alan was holding his vigorously shaking stomach with his left hand as we serenely headed northbound approaching Bellingham. Alan changed to the left lane because of a slow-moving large truck-and-trailer rig.

From my passenger window I glanced at the driver and for an instant we made eye contact. He had what looked like a grin on his face as he animatedly talked into his microphone. He was undoubtedly talking to a state patrol officer telling him about some idiot farmer with a sick cow he called Bessie, who had tipped his horse trailer while exiting the freeway a few miles back.

It seems that sometimes when you do tell it the way it is, no one believes you. Or if they do, they think you're more than a little crazy. Only Bessie knows for sure.

Pressures and Pranks

Humor is often the best medicine for depression.

My working days often exceeded sixteen hours, especially during the time of relentless stress while we were searching for ways to survive. I had worked so hard to build the businesses. Now they threatened to become lost in imminent bankruptcy. My family and employees relied on me to find a way for the business and paychecks to continue.

It was also at that time that an eye specialist, treating the loss of vision in one of my eyes, explained that it was his preliminary diagnosis that I had multiple sclerosis (MS) At that time I knew nothing about MS. What I heard from others I didn't like at all. Once my vision gradually started returning, I decided simply to ignore it.

Walking along the sidewalk from my home to my business, I remembered that Marty was to have connected the thin piano wire to a small screw eye fastened to the rear part of a desk drawer in the radio station office. Then he was to thread it through a couple of thin office wall dividers and place the end of the wire on the electronic service bench in the back of store. If done right, it would never be noticed.

Through the one-way window in my office I saw our radio advertising sales rep walk into the station office. I knew Barney's routine well. He would open his folder, remove any orders he had and separate the duplicate sheet, then hand one to Ilone, who was the advertising copywriter. He usually conveyed some specific client instructions

113

to Ilone. Then he would open the top drawer of his large wooden desk while still perusing his latest orders. While he was busy with that, I sneaked unnoticed to the service bench, which was out of sight of the broadcast station offices.

No one knew I was around. Simply watching the bolt attached to the end of the piano wire told me that Barney had just, almost absent mindedly, pulled his top desk drawer open while still concentrating on his order blanks. I gave the piano wire a mighty vigorous jerk. The "kapow" coming from Barney's office was initially like a gunshot but suddenly seemed to turn into an earthquake. Barney's order book flew high into the air along with his legs.

This placed the center of gravity of his office chair too far aft and in an instant Barney lay on the floor with his chair on top of him, letting out unearthly screams followed by bellowing: "HOLY COW, DID YOU SEE THAT!?"

Of course Ilone had seen that while letting out an extended high-pitched squeal. She shot off her chair like an arrow from a bow and commenced backing out of the confines of the office. By now she was undoubtedly certain that this was the beginning of the end of the world. Before they both saw me, I had silently raced back to my rear office.

Now I came storming out of the back yelling, "I heard all that noise. What's happening?"

I put a look of genuine concern on my face just as I entered the office. Barney was still on the floor, dazedly trying to wrestle the office chair off his stomach. Ilone stood, ashen faced, alternately staring untrustingly at the top drawer and poor Barney, who was still struggling to get himself right side up off the floor. I noticed that the small roller wheel on Barney's desk chair had hooked under his trouser belt.

That's why Barney had been struggling so valiantly to get the chair off his stomach without understanding why something so simple was impossible now. "Sid, the devil is playing with me," he said.

I felt a momentary pang of guilt. If whoever was playing with Barney was the devil, I was glad that I was the only one that knew who that devil was. I had to push Barney's stomach in to release the chair wheel from underneath his belt and help him to his feet.

He quickly extracted a pack of cigarettes from his pocket and attempted to light it nervously. It wouldn't work. His hand holding the lighter was shaking like a happy baby goat's tail. I took my matches and lit his cigarette.

"What in the world happened, Barney?" I asked. Still virtually speechless, he pointed to the closed top left drawer in his desk.

"It . . . it slammed shut. . . . all by . . . by itself."

"What? Barney, all by itself? That can't be." With that I slowly pulled the offending drawer open. Barney headed for the exit.

"Sid! Be careful. It banged shut so loud I thought the whole desk was exploding."

"Oh, come on, Barney. You don't believe in ghosts, do you?"

"No, Sid." He paused for a few seconds before adding, "I never did. But goodness gracious, I thought I was dead."

Ilone shook her head in vigorous agreement. I said, "Barney it's lunchtime. Why don't you take the afternoon off?"

"Ya," responded Barney. "And I need at least a full pint of Bourbon on ice."

My horn went crazy

The horn blows not at midnight but all the time.

One of our Motivating Sound background music parts suppliers had filed a lawsuit to collect the money we owed them. The papers were on my desk. It required a response. Our company had no money to hire a law firm to prepare an official response. Neither did we have a defense. We simply didn't have the money. I responded and explained that our best customer had declared bankruptcy, leaving us with thousands of dollars owed, which was now uncollectible.

"While we are doing everything in our power to avoid bankruptcy and satisfy our creditors over time, our chances of success are slim to zero," I wrote. I further wrote, "We respectfully request that your client send us an authorization to return, for credit, any new parts and components currently in stock.

"Since it is unlikely that we will be able to avoid bankruptcy, we have suspended the fabrication of background music equipment as well as our point-of-sale merchandiser units. Our business relations with your client firm have always been pleasant and it is with regret that I have to write this letter and plead for your understanding and cooperation." I put a stamp on the letter and placed it in the outgoing mail tray.

Dejectedly, I placed my chin on the palms of my hands and cupped my cheeks, staring through the one-way window overlooking the retail floor of our business. My emotions were churning in a turbulent sea of darkness in which I was completely submerged, but still looking for a small ray of light that could indicate that the surface of daylight was still within reach.

I heard the quick short footsteps coming from the direction of our now barely functioning electronic fabrication area. Steve was all excited. Steve didn't live by the clock or his watch. If he was developing some new electronic marvel, he'd likely work through the night. "Hey Sid, I got it all worked out and I think I should install it in George's green Subaru KLYN news car."

"Not so fast, Steve, What did you fabricate now."

He grinned and explained, "It's a device that connects to the horn in the car and as long as I or someone with this little remote—"

He pulled a square little aluminum box out of his pocket and pushed the spring-loaded activation button. "As long as I'm within about 300 feet I can honk the victim's horn. George's car is behind the building now and I'm going to install it while he's busy preparing the news."

George was the news director at KLYN. He was a pleasant young man and represented the radio station with skill and dignity.

Still excited, Steve continued. "When George goes for lunch, I'll follow him on my bike riding on the sidewalk."

"That'll be fun, Steve. I think Barry, Jim and I will go for lunch at the same time. Maybe stay just one or two cars behind George with our windows rolled down. I know he always goes to the Dutch Treat restaurant."

That afternoon George headed to the back of the building where the car was parked. Steve was already out of the door with his bike, armed with his wireless horn-activation device. Three of us headed out as soon as George had turned right on Front Street and was out of sight. All four of our windows were rolled down.

Steve was nonchalantly riding his bike along the sidewalk, weaving around pedestrians and adjusting his speed to the slow traffic pace George was maintaining. He also stayed out of sight of George even though that would not have tipped George off to the reality that a joke was about to be played on him.

He was only a recent employee and had no idea that he was among people with mischievous minds, of which his boss was chief. All he knew was that I was a serious, hard working man, totally lacking a sense of humor.

Suddenly, there it was: "Honk, honk, honk." Or more precisely a somewhat shrill, insistent, drawn-out "Tuut, tuuuut, tuuuuut." We strained our necks to get a glimpse of our victim. George was rapidly swiveling his head, looking from the button in the center of his steering wheel to the floor and out through the windows. The horn button didn't move by itself. He could see that. He surely wasn't touching it. He knew that.

Fortunately it quit as quickly as it had started and George made a left turn on Third Street. The light of the stop sign at Third and Grover was red. George had to stop. Two elderly ladies took advantage of the red light to cross the street right in front of George's car. Suddenly they stopped right in front of the green KLYN news car.

Their faces reflected raw panic as the horn of George's car blasted full force. The ladies were sure they were about to be run over by a car that must not have stopped at the red light. George raised both arms and hands and waved them vigorously as if in complete surrender, hoping that the poor petrified old ladies would recognize that he wasn't touching anything and was totally innocent of scaring them half to death. When George returned to the office in mid-afternoon, he told me all the details about his car horn going completely crazy. I listened sympathetically and innocently.

"Sid, I took the car to the Subaru dealer garage to check my horn."

I thought, Oh, my goodness; they found the small contraption Steve had installed.

"Did they find the problem, George?" I asked.

"No, they couldn't find anything wrong. They worked on it about 15 minutes. They charged it to KLYN. Here is a copy of the bill."

As soon as he left my office, I called my friend at the dealership and told them that if George came in again complaining about his horn blaring at the most embarrassing moments to tell him that his horn works fine.

"But, Ed, let me tell you a secret," I said. "We have installed a little device under the hood of the car. We can remotely activate his horn, and he doesn't know it."

Ed howled with laughter as he remembered how embarrassed George had been when two old ladies thought he was about to run them over. "Ed," I said, "he might come again because I think we are not finished with his horn yet."

George didn't know it, but he would have another surprise.

Poor vision but no blind spot

Hinshaw might be blind, but that didn't mean he couldn't see better than the rest of us.

I peered at the slightly fluorescent hands of the clock adorning our bedroom dresser. It was almost 2 a.m. I was now fully awake and drenched in perspiration. I sat up quietly, not wanting to disturb my dear wife Margaret. No, it wasn't a hot summer night. Suddenly my wet t-shirt felt cold and I slid under the blankets again. No matter how much I prayed for peaceful slumber, my mind raced in a thousand different directions, searching, hoping, and praying for some miracle that would avoid my company's as well as my personal bankruptcy. I had not yet fully learned that a mind under stress does not function well.

It disturbs the normal mental and physiological equilibrium of the brain and creates enormous physical and emotional strain and tension. Stress can have a paralyzing effect on our ability to think and react. As a pilot I had learned to treat stress with a calm, confident composure and never to panic. Panic leads to disaster.

Was I panicking now? Was I absolutely certain that relentless, non-abating stress would lead to experiencing increasing episodes of MS exacerbations resulting in ever increasing physical impairment? Yes, I was certain! Yes, I was scared, far more scared than you can imagine. Overwhelming fatigue was my constant companion, day and night.

In the distance I heard the sound of a car horn. Only my soundly sleeping Margaret kept me from laughing out loud when I recalled the image of poor George signaling to the old lady his total innocence of blowing his horn while she was in a crosswalk and the light was red. Soon I drifted off, bathing in the sweet relief of slumber.

A few hours later I became aware of a sliver of sunlight, visible between the drawn blackout bedroom curtains. Suddenly I was wide awake. There were vague memories of the nightmarish business failure thoughts and the drenching perspiration. Those negative thoughts were quickly banished and replaced with the image of two old ladies torturing our poor victim George with withering looks of disgust on their faces. All those wake-up sensations were topped by the realization that my fatigue had disappeared as mysteriously as it had arrived. I enjoyed a pleasant breakfast with Margaret and our children.

In the early afternoon my partner Rook and I had an appointment with a company in Vancouver, B.C. It was one of our clients and during an earlier meeting with the owner of the company I had hinted that we might consider selling our Vancouver operation. The man showed serious interest. He didn't know that a successful sale of our Vancouver operation was our only hope of preventing total failure and bankruptcy.

Not that we were deceiving him. His company had been an excellent dealer for our background music systems and we held Mr. Hinshaw, the primary owner, in high esteem. At times we felt sorry for him. At some point in his life he had lost the sight in one eye. His sight in his remaining eye must have been less than 20-20 because he was not allowed to drive. Always having his partner do the driving was a limitation for him. Our Canadian operation was an entity completely separate from our U.S. operation. The failure of our U.S. operation would not affect a new owner of the Canadian operation.

It was almost two o'clock in the afternoon when we arrived at the offices of our client, who was now our potential buyer of our entire

Vancouver inventory. I had drafted a simple asset-only purchase and sale agreement together with exclusive rights to distribute our products throughout the province of British Columbia.

Mr. Hinshaw introduced his two associates and then eagerly asked, "Mr. Baron, have you had an opportunity to prepare a contract?" I think that question revealed to both Rook and myself that our prospect was excited about consummating a deal.

"Yes, I have, Mr. Hinshaw. I didn't have an attorney draw up a complex legal document. We have done business with your company for quite some time, so I pretty much put in contractual form what you and I discussed on the telephone a couple of days ago."

"That's great," responded Mr. Hinshaw. "I am a firm believer in keeping things simple."

"Okay, gentlemen, I believe we're all on the same wavelength. The proposed contract is only three pages. All inventory items are listed and there is no cost allocated for the exclusive distribution rights. I have a copy for each of you. Take your time reading through it."

Mr. Hinshaw held the typewritten page very close to his nose and I could see his eye carefully scanning each line. It was nearly five minutes after the other two partners finished reading their copy before Mr. Hinshaw lowered his copy to his knee, smiled at me and said, "Mr. Baron, there isn't a blind spot in the whole contract."

I responded, "Gentlemen, we'll excuse ourselves to give you an opportunity to discuss it."

Hinshaw glanced at his two partners, who simply nodded silently. Quickly Hinshaw said, "Oh, no, gentlemen, that won't be necessary. We are ready to sign."

With that he passed the original copy to his partners and then he signed it himself. After exchanging some more details and pleasantries, he handed me a check and I handed him a key to our Vancouver rented office. I couldn't display the enormous sense of relief I felt. It wasn't until a few minutes later, when heading southbound on Canadian highway 99, that Rook grabbed my hand and shook it vigorously with congratulations. Then he started laughing.

It probably was mostly a release of pent-up fears and emotions, but I asked, "What are you laughing about, Rook?"

Still laughing, he looked at me and almost stammered, talking and laughing at the same time "Hinshaw's first name."

"Yes, Rook. I know. It's Charlie," I said. He nodded his head in apparent vigorous disagreement and unable to quit laughing stuttered, "No, it's Blindspot. Blindspot Hinshaw." Ever after we always referred to him as "Blindspot Hinshaw."

Actually, there was no clever, deceptive language in the contract. It was simple and straightforward. His company remained one of our clients.

New quandaries

The day I flew to Salem, Oregon, was memorable for two reasons. One was that my company made a big sale of its Motivating Sound tapes. The other was that I took part in a terrific practical joke.

The engine of my four-seat Piper Tri-Pacer aircraft purred steadily. Actually, "roared" would be a better description. It was downright noisy in the cockpit. I was alone at 3,000 feet, following the main highway to Salem. The Trojan nuclear power plant in was just off my right wing, on the bank of the mighty Columbia River.

The aerial map on my right knee told me that I was approaching the Portland area. I decided to fly slightly west of the city, to avoid having to ask Portland International Airport control for clearance to transit their airspace.

For the past two hours I had been gratefully contemplating the successful sale of our Vancouver distributorship inventory. Now we had enough funds to pay all of our obligations with even a small balance left over in our checkbook. So my thoughts turned instead to the telephone call I had gotten that morning. It had filled me with a sense of excitement; the anticipation of new challenges always did. On the outer edges of that excitement I could also sense the soft little voice of caution. I wanted to ignore it, but I felt a sense of trepidation that I couldn't fully ignore.

Bill Meyer was a good customer for our Motivating Sound background music. He lived in Salem, Oregon, and had been an electronic engineer at Advanced Technology Manufacturing Corp.—until cruel fate intervened.

That company designed and manufactured the first solid-state, handheld two-way radios. These were probably the forerunner of today's cellular phones with walkie-talkie features. Not long after they sold hundreds of units to the U.S. Forest Service and other agencies, it had become apparent that there was a problem with the transistors overheating. The units were all returned to the factory so that the transistor cooling and ventilation features could be redesigned. This had placed an enormous financial burden on the company. They were forced into bankruptcy. Bill then found himself out of work until an electronic equipment manufacturer in Minneapolis acquired the facility and began the design and development of an electronic point-of-purchase advertising system.

It was Bill who had called me that morning. I remembered the conversation quite clearly.

"Good morning, Sid." I recognized Bill's cheery voice immediately and could visualize him on the other end of the line in Salem. Bill was short in stature, but he was a giant in good manners, kindness, and integrity. His face was tanned with more wrinkles and creases than a person his age should normally have, probably as the result of many years of chain smoking. In an equally cheerful voice I responded, "Hi, Bill! How are things in the great capitol of the State of Oregon?"

"Things are going well here, Sid. And guess what? I need six more background music machines and twenty four music tapes."

Bill couldn't see me nod happily. He continued talking: "Sid, I think there may be an important opportunity for your company." Now he had really captured my attention.

"What's that, Bill"? I asked.

"The company from Minnesota wants to close their plant here and dispose of the inventory of used and work-in-progress units. Their point-of-sale merchandising units have been extensively and successfully field tested in grocery stores. As you know, they can integrate with your background music systems. This is a natural purchase for your company, Sid." I remained silent for several seconds. "Are you there, Sid?" asked Bill.

"Oh, yes, Bill. I'm here. Just trying to think. I agree it would be a perfect addition to our line of background music systems. We could possibly expand our distribution nationwide. It's just that we don't have the funds for a major investment like that."

Bill responded almost immediately. "I understand, Sid. Dennis Klinworth, the CEO and president of the parent company is a good friend. He's coming next week. He'll have dinner at our house and I'd like to invite you too."

"Thank you, Bill, that's very nice of you and your wife, but. . . ."

Bill interrupted me. "Why don't you get in your airplane, bring me the equipment and tapes, and I can show you the plant and inventory when you get here?"

So I did. Bill met me up at the airport in Salem and gave me the grand tour. Now I was on my way back and could see the nuclear power plant still visible over the left wing of the Piper. Flying an airplane requires constant attention, which includes frequent instrument scans, radio communications, and situational and location awareness, as well as constant vigilance for other air traffic, but my mind was in overdrive with excitement about the opportunities for expanding our business. Only occasionally did I allow the demons of negativism to enter my mind with thoughts of the peril that could very well be an ingredient of opportunity.

It wasn't until air traffic control advised that another airplane was southbound over the freeway just north of Chehalis at 3,000 feet that I snapped back to reality. I quickly acknowledged the transmission. I was flying at the same altitude as the other aircraft above the same highway heading in exactly the opposite direction! When I realized this

I instantly forgot about the clouds of possibilities and opportunities. A pragmatic inner voice told me that if I didn't concentrate on flying the airplane safely, there would be no possibilities or opportunities. A young widow with fatherless children could well become the tragic victim of my mental musings. So I came back to attention; tragedy was avoided. At seven in the evening the Tri-Pacer touched down safely at the Lynden airport. By ten in the evening I was happily perched in my favorite armchair, reading the Oregonian.

"Hey, honey, the phone is for you." It was the kind voice of my wife Margaret. I looked at the clock and realized how late it was. Who could that be, so late in the evening?

Cell phones were not yet available, so I put down my paper and crossed the room to reach the phone.

The voice on the other end belonged to my son Jim. "Hey, dad!" he exclaimed. I immediately detected excitement in his voice and, with a mixture of concern and curiosity, I said: "What's up, Jim?"

"We have George's car wired with the remote horn activation receiver," he told me. "Marty and I got it wired up this afternoon while George was recording part of his early morning newscast."

I was already giggling, because I could see what Jim was up to. Marty was another of our company technicians.

"You know, dad," Jim continued, "George goes to bed before ten because his shift at KLYN-FM starts early. He lives alone with his big German shepherd and he always parks his car close to the house, next to his bedroom window. Marty and I thought we'd give him a little serenade tonight." I giggled a little louder. "Marty borrowed a car from one of his buddies that George won't recognize, even if he pays attention to it. Dad, we'll pick you up in five minutes."

Twenty minutes later we were driving along Grover, in a tree-lined suburban neighborhood, heading for the house where George lived. When we got there, the rooms were all dark, the curtains drawn.

George's Subaru, emblazoned on both sides with the call sign and slogan for KLYN-FM was parked on the driveway close to a window. We parked our car directly across the street, with the engine shut down and the lights turned off. All three of us hunkered down in our seats so that we were completely invisible to anyone driving by or simply looking at our car.

Marty was in the driver's seat. Jim held the small battery-operated transmitter in his hand. All he'd have to do was hold it briefly above window level, point it directly at George's car, and press the button. That would activate George's horn. We watched the house carefully. There were no lights, no signs of movement. Clearly George and his dog were sound asleep.

All three of us, on the other hand, were wide awake. We took one last look up and down the street; no traffic was coming. We ducked our heads. Jim's hand went up. The little two-inch transmitter was barely visible at window level. Our windows were all rolled down. We didn't want to miss hearing the serenade.

The coast was clear. Jim pushed the button. There were two quick blasts from the horn of George's car, then three more short blasts. Now the quiet of the night returned while six eyes carefully peered over the edge of the open windows. A drape in the front window of the house moved, and George's head appeared. The curtain opened a little further and a large dog put his front paws up against the window and surveyed the seemingly deserted surroundings. Our heads went down again. While we stifled our laughter, Jim's hand carefully aimed the little transmitter again. This time there weren't just a couple of short honks. The horn blasted continuously for what seemed like a full minute. The lights came on, not only in George's house but also in the house next door. Jim released the button, and we carefully peeked out again.

The front door of the house opened. George appeared in his bathrobe, German Shepherd right on his heels. With flashlight in hand he examined the interior of his car. Finding nothing amiss, he walked around to the other side. When he was right in front of the car he turned his head to scan the surroundings. Suddenly two short blasts came from his horn. They clearly startled him. He ran to the driver side window. There was no one there who could have pushed the horn button on his steering wheel. He scanned his surroundings again. We quickly put our heads back down. Our car appeared dark and unoccupied. Then George went back inside. We waited a full five minutes before Marty started the car and we rolled up the windows as we drove away.

Just before noon the following day, George came up to me. "Sid, I've had it with that miserable car. Last night the horn kept going off all by itself. It kept me awake for hours."

"Oh, my goodness, George," I said. "I'm sorry. I don't know how something like that could happen."

"I don't know either, Sid, but it did. Last night was at least the third time. I took it to the garage again."

"Did they find the problem?"

"No, damn it! The mechanics just sit in the front seat, push the horn button and tell me that there's nothing wrong with it. When I tell them that it goes off in the middle of the night all by itself, they give me a silly grin and act like I've gone nuts."

I fought valiantly to suppress my own silly grin, but somehow managed to remain serious. "I'm sorry, George. That's embarrassing."

"You're darn right, it's embarrassing. I want another car."

This was getting serious, I thought. I was beginning to feel a twinge of guilt.

I scratched my head thoughtfully and said, "George, the radio station doesn't have the money to buy another car, but I'll tell you what I'll do. If that horn acts up one more time I'll buy you another car myself."

"Sid, is that a promise?" He looked startled by my generosity.

"That's a promise, George." He shook my hand vigorously. As he walked away he stopped, looked back and said: "You'd better start shopping, Sid."

Secretly I removed the receiver placed under the hood of George's car and took possession of the remote horn activator transmitter.

George's car horn never again tooted involuntarily.

Earthquake?

"Sid, I can tell that you're excited about the opportunity. Don't forget, it wasn't that long ago that we barely avoided bankruptcy." The speaker was my friend and business partner "Rook" Van Halm. My wife Margaret had said essentially the same thing earlier.

Both of them knew that I loved challenges. Both knew that the vision of unlimited opportunities was enormously attractive to me. They also knew that I was careful. I hated the idea of bankruptcy more than anyone else they knew. Both knew I would intensely analyze the risks and potential rewards.

"Yes, Rook. You're right. I didn't forget our close brush with bankruptcy. It's just that I see a fabulous opportunity here. When I balance the risk against the reward, I can see that there will definitely be risks. I can't be sure about the rewards. They might be even greater than we can imagine. The problem is, we're still operating on a shoe-string. We'll have a great product and no competition, but we're badly undercapitalized. On the other hand, if we want Motivating Sound, Inc., to become the kind of company we envisioned when we started it, we have to take advantage of this opportunity."

Rook nodded his head in serious contemplation. "Precisely what does the equipment do and how does it fit in with our background music equipment?"

"That's the beauty of it, Rook. It's a point-of-sale merchandising system. Up to ten small speakers can be attached to each unit. These little speakers are placed behind displays of items on grocery store shelves. The small cassette tapes have appropriate messages prerecorded on them. The solenoid-operated rotary switch in the unit will randomly select and activate one message at a time and send it to the appropriate small speaker in one of the displays. Imagine this, Rook: A shopper stops at the display of Grandma's Cookies. Suddenly a mystery voice explains that the chocolate chip variety of Grandma's Cookies has just been reduced in price by a full ten percent! Or a shopper looks at Johnson's Dog Food and hears the sound of a barking dog followed by a brief message about today's dog food special. Each message is localized and not transmitted over the storewide speaker system."

I could tell Rook's wheels were spinning. Then he started laughing. "What if the switch gets two locations mixed up?" he said. "You might have Johnson's dog barking in Grandma's cookies!"

We were both laughing now. I said, "You've got the picture, Rook. That's not a far-out example. But the company who made them has done a lot of research. They've had beta test sites in some very large chain grocery stores. They've accumulated a lot of documentation indicating significant success and satisfaction along with increased sales records of the items being promoted."

Rook looked impressed. "So these guys have done all the research and feasibility studies? Would we inherit that if we buy their inventory?"

"Absolutely, Rook. In fact, I wouldn't think of getting into it without that. All we'd need to do is assemble the unfinished units and begin marketing."

Rook didn't respond. He looked at me for several long seconds as if he wanted to see just which way the wheels in my cranium were turning. "I trust your judgment completely, Sid," he said.

"Thank you, Rook. I appreciate that." With that I turned and went back to my office. There was a lot to be done.

I was in the middle of a lengthy telephone conversation with a factory representative when Herm walked in. Herm sold advertising for KLYN. The look on his face told me that he was excited about something important.

Herm was short in stature, but that was not what people first noticed when they met him. They noticed his smile. It was so real, so genuine, that even when they first saw it, they couldn't help liking and trusting the man behind it. He was currently attending Western Washington University in Bellingham studying for a career in teaching, but for now his career was "sales."

I continued concentrating on my phone conversation. Subconsciously I thought that Herm might have closed a huge advertising contract. After I returned the telephone handset to its cradle, I swiveled my chair slightly to face Herm. Yes, the big smile was there. Yes, the twinkle in his eyes was there. But within that twinkle I detected something else, just a trace of naughtiness. Could he have learned that from his boss?

"Sit down, Herm," I said. He quickly settled into his chair and started telling me about the elaborate prank he had thought up. "Sid, we have an extensive sound effects library in our studio. When I was preparing a radio commercial for one of my good clients, I came across the sound effect of a crashing chandelier. That gave me a very naughty idea."

I nodded and grinned while Herm continued. "You know, Sid, my mom has this crystal chandelier hanging above the dinner table. She just loves that chandelier."

I quickly interrupted: "Herm, you can't break your mother's priced possession. Crystal chandeliers are very valuable. Also very fragile."

"Oh, no, no! I wouldn't break the chandelier. I'd only make her believe, maybe for a couple of minutes, that it's broken."

Now my curiosity was piqued and I asked: "How are you going to pull that off, Herm?"

"Well, see, my mom is at a cousin's house south of Mount Vernon today. She's coming back this afternoon. I have her cousin's telephone number. I think I have the whole episode in my head. I just need to transfer that crashing chandelier sound effect onto a little audio cassette and feed it directly into our phone line while I'm talking to her."

"That should work. You can even make a cassette recording of both sides of the conversation, including the sound effects."

"When can we do it?" Herm asked eagerly.

"Hey, time's a' wasting! Let's get moving on it now. I'll take care of the sound effect and I'll record the conversation for you."

Herm giggled audibly as we headed for the recording studio. It didn't take him long to find the sound effect we needed. The track he was looking for was on one of the 12" long-play vinyl records we kept in the library. It didn't take me more than a few minutes to transfer the 13-second track to a cassette tape. After cueing it up all I had to do was hit the play button at the appropriate moment. I nodded to Herm and he immediately started dialing a telephone number. I put on my headphones, which would allow me to hear both sides of the conversation. "Hi, Louise, this is Herm. Is my Mom there?"

"Yes, she is, Herm. Just a minute."

A concerned voice said: "Hi, Herm, is anything wrong?"

"No, there's nothing wrong, mom. I'd forgotten you were gone today. I just stopped by the house. Oh, hold on, what's this?" Herm's voice suddenly became excited. "Can you feel it in Mount Vernon, mom?"

"Feel what, Herm?"

"The house is shaking." There was mounting excitement in Herm's voice. "The whole house is rocking and rolling. The chandelier is swinging wildly. Oh, goodness. This must be an earthquake."

His voice had now risen to panic level. "Mom, I'm crawling under the table. This is so awful! The chandelier is starting to break loose from the ceiling. It's going to crash!"

He gave me a quick nod while I pushed the button. The telephone line filled with the sound of a crashing chandelier. Herm's mom's voice was now filled with panic. "Her . . . Her . . . Herm, are y-y-you all right?"

"Yes, mom, I'm all right. Everything is okay now."

"What do you mean, everything is okay? My crystal chandelier is totally destroyed. I heard it myself."

"No, mom, your chandelier is all right."

"Herm, what's the matter with you. I heard it plain as day over the phone."

"Mom, I was playing a trick on you. I'm at the radio studio. You heard a sound effect of a crashing chandelier."

There was almost total silence on the other end of the line, punctuated by rapid breathing. "Herman, you . . . you big mispunt!" The Dutch word meant pretty much the opposite of "sweet little boy." "If you weren't already grown up I'd put you in the corner for three days straight and send you to bed each night without supper!"

"Yes, mom, I understand. I would have deserved it. Sorry to scare the daylights out of you."

I wasn't sure he was really sorry, though. There was still a distinct twinkle in his eye. There was probably one in mine too.

Dilemmas in Dallas

It was hot as a very hot day in Texas.

And it seemed that on this trip the Devil Himself was in Dallas, ready to tempt me.

Coming from Holland and living in Washington State, I'm not exactly used to hot weather.

It was just before midnight when I took the elevator to the fourteenth floor of a big Dallas hotel. It had been a long two days in Dallas. I was beyond merely tired. I'd been away for a while, and I was longing for the comforting arms of a woman.

Alas, I well knew that a traveling businessman had options.

I was assisting our Texas Manufacturer Rep firm in contacting some of their clients who had expressed an interest in our Modern Merchandiser units.

Yes, it had been a grueling hot day. Just over 100 degrees Fahrenheit. After a two-hour call, we got into our car, which was parked in a hot asphalt parking lot. It was like squeezing into a hot oven.

It always took a few minutes before the car air-conditioning system reduced the temperature to a comfortable level. I had spent the entire day making calls with two key people from the firm representing our company, Motivating Sound, Inc.

Early in the evening my business associates and I drove to a fancy restaurant for a nice dinner. The two men I had worked with all day were used to spending evenings in bars and restaurants. The life of a sales rep was a traveling life five days a week.

They were both in their mid-to-late thirties and returned to their wives and families every weekend. Their sales territory covered three states, including Texas. Dallas was their home city and the headquarters of their firm.

Now we were sitting in the restaurant lounge ordering the first round of drinks. The night before I had already learned that it was their custom that each member of the party orders a round for all in turn. Of course this meant that I too had to order a round of drinks. Perhaps to celebrate a successful business day, it wasn't until after the third round of drinks that dinner was suggested.

Fortunately I'd always had a strong dislike for the effects of alcohol. As soon as I could tell that something was beginning to feel a little woozy in my head I'd had enough.

In deference to my hosts I needed to do some fancy faking to still be one of the boys. But I was sober. Whenever they looked at me or asked me a question, I took a sip. When their attention turned to the game on the lounge TV, the puddle under my chair expanded a little. I was not unfamiliar with the average lifestyle, customs and morals of traveling salesmen. For that reason I wasn't too surprised when they asked if I wanted them to arrange for a sleeping companion for me.

And I have to say, I felt the Devil's hot breath in my ear.

In my briefcase was an order for sixteen of our electronic Modern Merchandiser units. It was the first order for the inventory we had acquired from the defunct Salem, Oregon factory. I tossed my briefcase on the bed. I pulled off my jacket and tie and sank in the deep-cushioned chair. The previous week I had spent several days at the Commercial Electronic show at the huge McCormick place in Chicago. My vision of building Motivating Sound, Inc., into a successful nationwide corporation had not been an idle pipe dream. With the help of competent people it could be within reach. Except, that is, for adequate capitalization. We did not have that. But there was something else. Something so important, that a virtual tornado of conflicting thoughts tumbled through my consciousness. I needed time to think.

Here I was, nearly two weeks away from my family, chasing the dream of unlimited opportunities. What was I sacrificing? What was I gaining? What would I be losing?

Yes, I could sleep with a strange woman tonight. That might be exciting. But years ago I had promised to be a faithful husband to Margaret Tjoelker. That was a promise. That was a commitment. Promises and commitments are not meant to be broken. I had never slept with a woman other than my dear, faithful wife Margaret. She was a wonderful wife and mother. No, she did not deserve a deceitful, unfaithful husband. What about my children? I loved them dearly. Was I now willing to trade being a fulltime father for the lure of greatness and gold in business success? What was more important? Or could I have both? What about my health? I had the incurable disease of MS. I was subjecting myself to enormous stress. It could worsen and even disable me very quickly.

I needed to talk to my Heavenly Father. I did that frequently, tonight especially, to calm the turmoil of my mind. I needed the guidance of the Holy Spirit.

With that I went to bed.

❋ ❋ ❋

The airplane was at its cruising altitude of 36,000 feet heading for Seattle. It was a smooth flight, not a cloud in the sky, not a trace of turbulence. It was in perfect harmony with the peace and tranquility I felt deep within. It was in stark contrast to the emotional turbulence I had experienced the night before. I don't know the many ways the Holy Spirit can work in the lives of people who search and seek divine guidance. As I watched the peaceful landscape slowly recede, I knew I had the answer to all the questions I had wrestled with the night before.

A few hours later I heard the chirp-chirp of rubber contacting the asphalt runway and I marveled at the captain's ability to "grease" this huge, heavy aircraft smoothly onto the runway at Sea-Tac airport. After a cab ride from Sea-Tac to the Boeing airport I climbed into my Piper Tri-Pacer and headed for Lynden—for home and for the most important people in the world, my family.

God had answered my prayers that night.

He'd blessed me with slumber before I could do anything stupid.

Hot Coffee at the PNE

My brother-in-law Wayne, comfortably seated by the table in our living room, looked at me and broke out in hilarious laughter. He was a tall, handsome man, and laughter came easily for him.

"Man, I wished we could have caught up with that cranky old guy again after we were finished at the police station."

I started laughing all over again. "Yes, Wayne, I'm sure you could have pushed his buttons again to send him into orbit one more time." There, amidst the comforts of cushions, drinks and the blissful aromas of home, we were reminiscing about an amusing event.

Margaret and I, along with my sister Greta and her husband Wayne, who were vacationing at our house from Michigan, had decided to spend an afternoon at the big Pacific National Exhibition in Vancouver, British Columbia. When we got there, we headed for the large roller coaster.

We watched the reactions of the brave riders as the cars chugged laboriously toward the summit. That was the calm and serene part of the ride. We wondered if the cars' occupants knew that their experience was about to change dramatically. After making a wide, lazy, level turn it suddenly changed direction and went into a screaming high-speed dive, followed by a hairpin turn that would have tossed the riders clear out of their seats if they were not securely strapped in. Above the noise of clattering metal on metal we could hear the occupants scream, some with sheer terror and others with great delight.

"Let's do it, Sid," Wayne urged.

I didn't want to let him know that I was almost too chicken to venture onto that steel monster on rails, so I nodded my head up and down.

Our wives told us that they were not about to join us.

We agreed that they should go their separate ways and we agreed to meet again in about two hours at a predetermined location.

Now it was early evening and we sat cozily around the table in our living room reminiscing about the events of the day.

"Yes, Wayne." I said, still laughing, "I'll never forget that crazy older fellow at the fair."

"That's for sure," said Wayne. "I can't imagine why the old goat wanted to go to the fair and be among thousands of people when he obviously hated to be in a crowd."

"What happened, honey?" Greta asked.

Both Greta and Margaret looked expectantly at Wayne, waiting to hear the story. With a big grin on his face, he answered.

"We mixed with a lot of other fairgoers and wormed our way through a number of buildings with all kinds of exhibits."

"None of those exhibits was as interesting as what was to come," I interjected.

Greta and Margaret looked at us with increasing curiosity. Impatiently Greta said, "C'mon, honey, tell us what happened."

With a wide grin and an expression that said "Wait till you hear this" on his face, Wayne continued.

"Sid and I worked our way through a huge exhibition building that was really crowded with people. Suddenly Sid gave me a bump and said, 'Look at that old fellow'."

I quickly chimed in again. "He was sitting at a table in a small eating area. His table was very close to the crowded walkway of the exhibition building. He had two fingers holding the ear of his coffee cup.

One of the ladies inadvertently bumped his table only slightly and a little coffee spilled."

"Is that what got the old goat so excited?" asked Wayne. I nodded and Wayne went right on.

"I saw him literally leap off his chair, yelling something at a couple of ladies who quickly disappeared in the crowd of people." He was obviously hopping mad that someone had bumped his table but knew that giving pursuit and trying to find the culprits in the crowds, would be an exercise in futility. With eyes still blazing in anger he turned to see if he could still find the two women that were somehow the cause of his sudden wrath before he sat down at his table again. Then Sid poked me again." I nodded somewhat guiltily, not wanting all the blame for what happened next.

"Well, Wayne," I said, "I just suggested that we sit down for a cup of coffee close to this interesting fellow."

"Oh, sure, Sid, you would never think of pulling a trick on a poor unsuspecting victim," Wayne said with a skeptical grin on his face.

"Okay, Baker," I responded. "The man had just bought a fresh cup of coffee. I was the one who suggested you go to the service counter and order us some coffee and one of those big chocolate chip cookies. But you didn't need much prompting. If I remember right you had the idea of bumping the old guy's table on your way back with our order."

Wayne's grin had turned to laughter. "Oh, my goodness, man, that was the start of it, all right," he said. Truly impatient now, with mounting curiosity, his wife gave him a good poke and said, "Hey, Baker." (She called her husband by his last name only when she was getting impatient with him.) "Go on. Tell us what happened," she pleaded.

"Okay, with both hands filled with two cups of hot coffee and two giant cookies, I bumped his table and sat down. I was only sitting about eight feet from him, but I couldn't see his reaction because I had my back turned toward him. I just watched Sid's face. His expression would tell me how the old man had reacted."

"That's right, Wayne," I responded. "You didn't bump his table very hard. His coffee didn't spill and he wasn't holding his coffee cup but was just turned around looking at the long line of people. He was probably still looking for those two evil women who had spilled his coffee and caused him to have to buy a fresh cup. He simply didn't notice that you bumped his table."

"Well, I took care of that in a hurry," said Wayne.

"Okay, Baker, what did you do?" asked Greta.

"Hon, I got up to pick up a little sugar bag. I turned around to return to my chair and 'accidentally' bumped his table pretty good. I sat down and watched Sid's face."

"You were barely seated, Wayne, when you knew something was happening, weren't you?" Wayne laughed.

"Oy, oy, man your eyes got as big as saucers. You didn't have time to say anything, but your expression was screaming alarm." Both Margaret and Greta were all ears now.

"Go on, hon, what happened?" asked Greta. Wayne didn't need urging and he quickly continued. "The next thing I knew a scalding hot cup of coffee splashed onto the back of my neck and sprayed pretty much everybody sitting in the small eatery."

Both Margaret and Greta's mouths fell open as they envisioned the indignity of getting hit with hot coffee in the neck.

As Wayne began to laugh again at the memories of what happened next, I quickly carried on. "Wayne, you shot out of your chair like a mermaid would have shot out of an alligator pond. You turned around and saw the old fellow quickly attempting to flee among the throng of people and you yelled, "Sid, let's go get him.""

"You bet," said Wayne. "I wasn't gonna let the old fart get away."

"You sure didn't, Wayne," I said.

"I had to work hard to stay right on your heels as you aggressively pushed your way through the crowd, never leaving the target out of your sight. The crowd thinned as we exited the crowded building. In a moment you grabbed him by the shoulder and took up position on his left. He grumbled some unintelligible words but didn't seem too surprised at his 'arrest.' I held him by the left arm and you had a firm hold on his right arm." Now our wives started laughing hard at the vision of little Sid and tall Wayne walking through the PNE grounds with a little old man between them.

"That must have looked like Mutt and Jeff," croaked Greta. "Man, I wished we had seen that. What did you do with him?"

"We marched right along and Sid asked him why in the world he went to the PNE with its thousands of fairgoers when he obviously hated crowds."

"What did he say?" Greta asked, looking at me. I quickly responded.

"He looked shiftily from Wayne to me and back to Wayne again all the while mumbling words we couldn't understand. He was probably worried silly wondering where we were going to take him and what we were going to do with him or to him. We marched him right over toward the PNE Police and Security station, which we had spotted in the distance."

"We barged right into the office still holding onto our "criminal," continued Wayne. There were two Vancouver police officers and at least two PNE security officers watching our little parade enter the station."

"What did you say?" our wives wanted to know. "I told them that this fellow had thrown scalding hot coffee all over me and showed him the red spots on the back of my neck and the coffee stains on my jacket.

I think the officers were skeptical even before any explanation was offered. Here were two young fellows dragging into the police station a little old fellow who was nearly a foot shorter than the shorter of the two young fellows. It looked suspicious, but they could see that the back of my neck had been overheated by something and that my jacket was stained with something other than what might have come from a seagull. They looked at the little old fellow. "What did he say, hon?" Greta wanted to know. Wayne thought for a moment and looked at me.

"It went something like this," said Wayne. "When the cop asked him what he had to say, he began to mumble something like this: 'Dem a-guys dem a dump me cuffee. Me-a cuffee it a spill. Dem a guys' and he pointed right at me and corrected himself. 'Them a tall a guy, he donna dit it.'"

I nodded my agreement as Wayne was recalling what the man had said and interjected, "The man was definitely not a native Canadian."

Wayne continued: "The officers looked at each other, then from us to the accused, and really didn't know what to make of it. It was at about that moment that the two women literally burst through the station office door. They had clearly been running and were huffing and puffing and very excited. They were carrying their jackets and almost immediately and simultaneously yelled, 'That's him. That's the guy.' They were pointing at the little fellow, who was still doing his best to defend himself from the accusations of 'Mutt and Jeff.' The course of events changed immediately. One officer spoke up firmly: 'Okay, ladies, calm down and tell us what happened.' The two women were very angry. They virtually yelled in unison, 'Officer, this guy threw hot coffee all over our clothes and us. Look at the coffee stains all over our jackets. He's going to have to pay for the cleaning bills.' The officer examined both of the ladies' jackets. He nodded and asked the ladies if they wanted to file charges. There was no question in the officer's mind that the ladies both responded in the affirmative. First the defendant had to provide them with his name and address and sign the form after the officer read him the charges. Then the old man was free to go. He would be hearing from the court later. The two ladies were also handed the paperwork. We told the officer that we were from the U.S. and did not want to press charges. We were now also free to go and quickly headed out of the door. Sid, looking in every direction, said, 'Where did he go? We could at least give him a farewell serenade of sorts and escort him from the PNE grounds.' We never saw him again."

That living room resounded with our laughter.

I can hear that sweet sound to this day.

Milking my Goat

Walking slowly had never been my style.

Now I walked the sidewalk from 525 to our home at 211 Front Street. I walked slowly.

I was bone tired. At 46 years of age I should still be immune to getting tired. But this wasn't just weariness. It was an overwhelming fatigue that all people with multiple sclerosis are very familiar with. I could no longer deny that I had MS nor that stressful days easily triggered new symptoms of the disease.

It had been a stressful day, not as much physically as emotionally. I didn't have to pack and load all remaining inventory, including partially completed background music players and Modern Merchandiser units. I only needed to say farewell to our Motivating Sound, Inc., business division.

How much easier it would be to simply load a bunch of equipment in a truck as opposed to presiding over the end of ten years of energies and efforts, tireless labor, day and night. To consciously recognize a failure and say farewell to years of ambitious efforts, of hopes and dreams and aspirations, is far more stressful than a good day of physical labor. Now I could wallow in the pity of it all and gradually destroy my restless spirit, or I could laugh at my temporary failure and build new hopes and dreams and visions of a bright future and unlimited opportunities still. Subconsciously I could not completely subdue thinking about the possibility of being totally incapacitated by ravishing Multiple Sclerosis.

Subconsciously my walking pace picked up. It wasn't until I walked up the three steps onto the front porch that I noticed we had company. Margaret was preparing a big dinner. Sons Jim and Gerald together with their wives, Laurie and Lynne, were visiting and staying for dinner.

Suddenly the blues of the day faded away as I counted the blessings of the solid unshakeable anchors in my life. Those anchors comprised my faith and my wonderful wife and family. Maintaining those solid anchors was far more important than the successful creation of a little empire I had been striving to achieve.

Hey, a little fatigue? I wasn't even going to talk about it. Self pity wouldn't help any more than pity of family and loved ones. I enjoyed the harmonious chatting as the family was seated around the table waiting for mother to put the finishing touches on another delicious meal.

That's when the telephone rang. Barely into its third ring, I picked up the handset with a cheery "Hello."

This was before the days of "caller ID." It was also before the days of restricted marketing calls.

"Is this Mr. Baron?" the female voice asked. The way she pronounced my name, I knew it wasn't one of my neighbors calling. The still present naughtiness of youth surfaced again and I decided to play this "marketing call" for all it was worth.

"Ya, diis ies Mr. Baaron, all right. Who are you?" I asked.

"My name is Gussy. I'm with National Beautification Services. We are going to have a truck in your area next Thursday and we would like to put brand new siding on your house. All for free."

"Ooh, man, dot ies fontostic," I said and continued, "Kin you shpeek op a liettle. I half an ol bottery phone. And I don heer so prutty good."

"Is this better?" she almost yelled.

"Ooh, ya, dos good now," I said.

She continued. "Are you still living at 211 Front Street?"

"Ya, shure," I said.

"Our truck will be there next week, Thursday. There's only an initiation fee of $100.00. Shall we put that on your credit card?" she asked. I knew she would ask for my credit card number next but I wasn't going to give her a chance."

"Ooh, dot wood be good," I said, quickly continuing, "Ya, you know, me phone. Botteries and no wires. I like dot. I kin go outside whiz it and half me phone right whiz me when I milk me goat on de lawn." Gussy remained quiet for a short while. I imagine she rarely encountered such a talkative, agreeable old man in her marketing calls. Besides, she had a deal. All she needed yet was the man's credit card number. The family members around the table were valiantly trying to subdue their laughter. Probably semi-disgusted with their "elderly" father, already in his mid forties, and his crazy antics. She must have recovered, because she now asked: "Sir, do you have a Mastercard or Visa?"

I said: "Ooh, it a Fisa, but wait, me goats jus' come on de lawn. Se want to be milked right away. I take me phone wiz me while I milk de goat." Gussy was quiet again. I think she covered her mouthpiece while she laughed. I quickly covered my mouthpiece too and loudly whispered to Jim to slam a door and Jerry to hit a pan with a wooden handle. Then I continued talking to the lady on the phone. "Goossey, I haff me pail and me milk stool and me phone between me shin and de shoulder." Again, silence. I quickly filled the void and sternly said: "Lula stand still." Lula was my imaginary goat.

"Are you still there, Goosey?" I asked into the phone.

Gussy's voice was a little shaky with laughter, but she said "Yes, Mr. Baaren, I'm here. I need your Visa card numb. . . ."

I quickly cut in. "Lula, get your dirty leg out of me milk pail."

The silence now seemed to last a full minute until I asked, "Goosey, you still wiz me?"

"Yes, sir, I'm still here. Do you have your credit card with you there?"

"Ya, Goosey, I haff it wiz me. Hang on a minute."

"Okay, Mr. Baaren, take your time." All I did for the next minute or so was breathe audibly, just so Gussy would know I had not abandoned her. Then I suddenly started yelling into the phone with an angry voice, "Hey Lula, you miserable old goat. You pooped in me pail." Now our dinner company quickly fled the room, unable to contain their laughter any longer. I carried right on: "You no good rotten old goat. Now ve cannot drink de milk any more. It look like chocolate milk. I give de pail to me wife. She can still sjurn it and make a little butter out of it. Maybe a little sheez."

I never heard Gussy's voice again.

I hung up. Gussy never knew that she had talked to a man who learned to milk a goat before he was ten years old.

I had a fun-filled, delicious dinner with my family.

My fatigue of the day completely left me.

The toilet flushes prematurely

Gradually at first, then very swiftly, my mind returned to consciousness.

Where was I?

Oh, yes. I was safe and sound in my own bed.

I was awake and looked at the clock radio on the dresser. It was 2:35 in the morning. Margaret, beside me, was sound asleep. I was glad she was sleeping.

Otherwise she would have asked if I had wet the bed.

Actually, I sort of had.

I was drenched in perspiration. Not only my night clothing but also part of the bedding was wet as well. Fully awake now, I became aware of strange sensations throughout my body. While these were different from previous undesirable sensations, I couldn't worry about that now. I needed the rest of slumber.

Tomorrow would be a very long and busy day.

For many weeks I had been promoting a Thomas organ concert in the largest auditorium in Lynden. Bob Ralston, who appeared every week on the nationally televised Lawrence Welk show, would play and demonstrate the various models of Thomas organs that we would have to haul to the stage prior to the evening concert. I had left no stone unturned to make sure that the nearly 1,000 seat auditorium would be filled.

Finally I fell asleep again. It was nearly 8 o'clock when I awoke. I dressed hurriedly, ate little, and raced off to the business.

Early in the afternoon I dragged my weary body into the house.

Margaret looked at me and immediately asked, "What's the matter?" It was not my custom to come home in the middle of the day. But that wasn't the only reason she asked the question.

"You're not feeling well," she said. She didn't have to phrase it in the form of a question. She could tell at one glance. I smiled feebly and sank down on the couch. I didn't really want to talk about the nasty messages my body was sending me.

"You're sick," Margaret said. "I can see it in your pallid face color. What are you smiling about?"

"I was thinking about the trick Marty played on Nellie," I said. "You know, Nellie gives piano lessons in one of our soundproof studios. A couple of days ago Marty, who is one of our electronics technicians, told me that he had ingeniously rigged the toilet for remote flushing."

With half a smile on her face, Margaret said: "See, there you have it already. You've played so many nasty tricks on people, now your employees are getting into it also. If too many customers get wind of all the trickery going on at 525 Front Street, they'll be afraid to come into our place of business."

"Yes, honey, you have a point. We just won't tell anybody," I said. She asked, "What happened to Nellie?"

I giggled a little and said, "I was sitting at my desk double checking the number of tickets we had distributed for the concert tonight. You know, Nellie is a very proper lady. She is reserved, always dresses very nicely and carries herself as a woman with a good measure of self-esteem. Of course she has every reason to feel good about herself. She is a well-known highly regarded pianist who graduated from the world-renowned Juliard School of Music in New York."

"Yes, I know," said Margaret.

"What happened?"

"She came up behind me and quietly said that she never speaks with a loud voice. She said, 'Mr. Baron?' She never calls me Sid. I swiveled my chair around to face her. Her face was red and she looked very embarrassed."

"What did she say?" Margaret wanted to know.

"She said, 'Mr. Baron, the toilet flushes all by itself'. Instantly, I made the connection to what Marty had told me, but I couldn't let on to Nellie. Instead I put a disbelieving look on my face and said, 'How would that be possible?' Nellie said: 'I don't know how it is possible. I just know that it did.'

"'Were you in the bathroom when the toilet flushed all by itself?' I asked.

"She looked at the floor, turned halfway around so as not to face me anymore, and while shifting her weight from one foot to another she said, 'I was sitting on the toilet when it flushed all by itself.'"

The serious expression on my face did not betray my inward laughter.

"'Oh, Mrs. van Wiksom,' I said. 'You probably inadvertently hit the little flush lever,' I said.

"More assertively now she responded, 'Definitely not. I would never have done that because I was not finished yet when it flushed.'

"It was getting more difficult now to maintain my composure, but I managed and said, 'Mrs. van Wiksom, I'm sorry about the flushing problem. I'll check it out myself in just a few minutes.' She turned to return to her piano student. Then she halfway turned back again and with a very embarrassed look on her red face, she said, 'When I got finished it wouldn't flush.'"

Margaret wasn't in the mood for amusement. Instead she looked at me with concern and said: "Something is wrong with you, isn't it?"

I nodded wearily. "What is it now?" she asked. "I'm sure it's another exacerbation of MS," I said, "but this is different and scary. It's not only the 'down to the core' fatigue, but in addition I'm getting numb from head to toe."

My dear wife sat beside me on the couch, kissed me on the cheek, and said, "Did you feel that"? I grinned and said, "No, do it again."

I explained to her that my sensation of numbness was more prominent on the left side of my body than on the right side and most prominent in my left hand and fingers. Also, that the numbness did not mean the absence of "feeling." My skin was still sensitive to touch and feeling. When I held my hand under cold running water, I would immediately notice as the water turned to warm and hot. Similarly, if I held a coin in my hand I could, without looking, determine if it was a penny, a dime or a quarter.

"But Margie" I said, "This is such a bad time. Bob Ralston and his wife are coming and we have almost 1,000 confirmed reservations for the concert tonight. I can barely drag my body around."

My wife looked at me. The expression of deep concern never left her face. "You've got to go to bed, honey. You can get somebody else to introduce Bob Ralston," she said.

"Yes, I'm going to rest for awhile, but I don't have anyone that can go on stage and introduce Bob Ralston of the Lawrence Welk show. Besides, we have to take him and his wife out for dinner tonight."

Margaret sat quietly staring at the floor. Slowly, she raised her head and we made eye contact as she spoke: "Sidney, listen to me." When she called me 'Sidney' I knew it was time for me to pay attention. "You know, hon, your life is my life. You know I'm deeply worried. I think you're worried also, although you have an amazing ability to cover it up." I didn't respond. I stared at the floor and listened intently. Margaret continued: "You've had MS for six years. You've had numerous symptoms. You've been in the hospital several times with infections. They give you some antibiotics, and soon you're well again. Except you still have MS. You lose vision in one eye; you pull off the highway and come to a full stop. We stay there silently for several minutes. Then your 'dizziness' disappears and we continue along the free-way. With each exacerbation you've experienced during the past six years, you've laughed and humored your way into remissions. The first urinary tract infection you had was very serious. Even while shaking with high fever you started writing a funny story. I think you called it 'Balls of Fire.' It was so funny I showed it to Doctor Webster. He almost fell off his swivel stool laughing. He wanted a copy to take to his upcoming medical convention. But honey," she continued, "here's what I'm afraid of. You have multiple sclerosis. If you keep up your complicated, hectic life of work and pressure, I fear that no amount of humor and laughter can ultimately shield you from the potentially devastating and totally destructive potential of ravaging, incurable MS."

I looked at my wife with loving admiration and said, "I didn't know you knew all that but you are absolutely right. I did some research last week in an effort to locate the most knowledgeable expert on MS. I knew we would go anywhere in the world to consult this expert. Much to my surprise I found that the world-renowned expert I was searching for had recently retired as head of the Department of Neurology at the University of Oregon Medical Center. His name is Roy L. Swank, MD, Ph.D."

Now Margaret was listening intently and I continued: "I'm not able to get out of our commitments this evening. Somehow, I think I'll get through it and nobody will even notice that MS is nibbling at me. But on Monday we have an appointment to see Dr. Swank in Portland at about noon."

Again, my wife planted a kiss on my cheek.

Yes, fun and laughter help relieve stress in the workplace.

But the greatest joys in your life are your relationships with loved ones.

The End

Addendum

Survive MS? That's what you read on the back-cover of this book. It requires an explanation because, as you read through the various chapters of the book, you may think that, with all the fun and laughter, I probably never really had MS. You be the judge.

It started when vision in my left eye became very blurry. I went to my optometrist who said: "You have a scratch on your eye. It should be better over the weekend."

Over the weekend I lost most of the vision in my eye. On Monday I returned to the optometrist. After examining the eye he said, "The scratch is gone. It should be OK now." When I told him that I had lost most of my vision in that eye, it didn't take him long to confirm that. Somewhat alarmed he said: "You have a serious problem and I can't help you. I will make an emergency appointment with a medical eye specialist." Less than two hour later I was sitting in a darkened examination room while the doctor and a nurse were partially removing my eyeball to gain access to the optic nerve into which they injected a cortisone shot. It wasn't a pleasant experience. After getting my eyeball in place again the doctor said:

"Mr. Baron, it has been my experience that the vision problem you are experiencing is, in most cases, one of the first symptoms of Multiple Sclerosis. I am writing a note to your family doctor and recommend certain tests that might eliminate other possible causes of your problems." He handed me the note to give to my family physician and send me on my way home.

"Oh my goodness honey, what happened to you?" After I quickly looked in a mirror and saw my thoroughly blood-shot eye, I could understand my wife's alarmed reaction.

It marked the beginning of spinal tabs and many other tests to eliminate other possible causes of the anomalies my body was exhibiting. I didn't know anything about MS. Sometime later a neurologist predicted that I would likely be in a wheel chair within ten to fifteen years. I remember thinking: 'not if I can help it doc'.

When my vision gradually improved, I decided to ignore the mysterious episode and fully concentrate on my career paths again.

A few short years later I could no longer ignore the multiplying problems that began to increasingly worry and puzzle me. There were episodes of momentary mental confusion and brief, strange episodes of dizziness. For the first time in my life I began to feel tired in a way I had never experienced being tired before. It would still be there after I awoke from a night of sleep and rest.

I learned later that MS patients are very familiar with fatigue. It's an overwhelming, aching feeling of being more than just tired. Long rests may not even be of much help. Especially not during periods of intensification of MS symptoms commonly referred to as 'exacerbations'. Numbness and sensory distortions invaded my body from head to toe. Parts of my body would feel hot, others cold. Even wearing wool lined leather gloves helped little in making my hands feel comfortable. Urinary track infections became frequent and landed me in the hospital on more then one occasion.

I simply could no longer ignore the fact that I had a very serious affliction for which every medial expert had told me, there was no known cause. There was no cure. Certain medications would be prescribed at times to alleviate some of the discomforts that always accompanied periods of intensification of the disease. At that point I could have busied myself with catalogs featuring wheel chairs. But I didn't. I wasn't going to yield to a mysterious disease capable of totally incapacitating my body. Not yet. Instead, after a particularly serious case of infection, I wrote about my experiences.

It was entitled: "Balls of Fire". Margaret took it to our family doctor. He found it hilarious and took a copy to take to his physician convention. It was good for many healthy laughs.

You see, if I was going to give in to ever increasing exacerbations with ever increasing deficiencies and handicaps, I certainly wasn't going to give up without a real fight. I also firmly believed that it's what God would have wanted me to do. I would constantly and fervently pray for divine blessings in my battle against the disease. I decided to do some research and find an expert specializing exclusively in Multiple Sclerosis. Margaret and I would make an appointed regardless of where in the world his office location might be. We discovered that the Neurologist who had devoted his entire career to the research and treatment of MS was right in our neighboring State of Oregon. He had recently retired as head of the Department of Neurology at the University of Oregon Medical center. But he did not retire. Instead he opened a modest office on the campus on the University where he would only see MS patients.

I remember my first visit to Dr. Swank very clearly. It was a Monday. I had a serious case of fatigue, numbness from head to toe on the entire left side of my body, and serious sensory distortion in both hands. Only my sense of humor was intact.

It was almost noon when Margaret and I arrived at his office. After exchanging some small talk he looked at his watch and said: "Why don't you go down to the cafeteria and have yourself a nice juicy big hamburger because it's the last juicy, fatty hamburger you should eat. As Margaret and I ate some lunch in the basement cafeteria, Margaret said, "My guess is that Dr. Swank's treatment is going to have something to do with diet." About 45 minutes later we were comfortably seated across the desk of Dr. Swank.

He asked me some questions and I described the various symptoms I had already experienced. Now he knew, beyond the shadow of a doubt, that I had Multiple Sclerosis. A clinical examination was not required to confirm that fact. I had MS.

"Unfortunately there is neither a known cure nor known cause of MS." Somewhat despondent I lowered my head only to suddenly raise it again and looking Dr. Swank squarely in the face I said "Dr. Swank if you cannot describe a medical regimen for MS patients to follow, why are you widely known as the most knowledgeable expert on the disease? Why should I have come to consult you?" He did not resent the bold manner in which I asked that question.

Instead Dr. Swank smiled. "Sid," he said. "I'm not surprised you ask that question because it reflects characteristics typical of most MS patients." "What are those characteristics?" I asked.

"Most MS people are impatient, intelligent and result oriented. They don't want to waste time and like to cut right to the chase. They're generally type A personalities, ambitious, responsible with strong leadership qualities. They tend to hold themselves to high standards in everything they do." "Wow, Dr. Swank," I said, "You almost make it sound as though I should be proud to have MS."

"Yes Sid, except that those characteristics, while largely positive, have one huge negative." Eagerly I asked, "What's that?" His answer came without a moment's hesitation. "People with those characteristics expect much of themselves, and often place themselves under unrelenting stress. It is often a major contributor to the frequent bouts of exacerbations most MS patient experience."

Dr. Swank explained that his research and treatment of MS patients started at the Montreal Neurological Institute in 1948 and that he devoted his entire life to the treatment and research of Multiple Sclerosis. Margaret and I listened quietly and intently.

Dr. Swank continued, "Now Sid I know you would like me to prescribe some magic potion or wave a magic wand and make your MS disappear, but I can't."

With a trace of disappointment in my voice, I asked, "Is there anything you can do?"

"There is very little I can do" the doctor said, "but I can tell you what you can do for yourself. If you follow the program I've developed over many years of research and have been proven to be effective for many hundreds of patients who agreed to be part of our research program."

I repositioned myself in the chair and said, "Dr. Swank, I know that most people, when they visit their physician, expect the doctor to prescribe whatever medication will cure their disease or at least diminish their discomfort. I've already read enough about MS that I know it's an incurable disease. If there's anything I can do for myself, I will do it!"

Dr. Swank smiled and nodded approvingly. He got up, walked over to a bookshelf in his office and picked up a thick, hard cover copy of a book entitled "The Swank MS Diet Book". Margaret and I had already speculated that Dr. Swank's program would have something to do with diet. Since Margaret is the cook in our family she knew immediately that the weight of implementing and complying with a restrictive diet would fall squarely on her shoulders.

"Sid," Dr. Swank continued, laying the book in front of me on his desk; "this is the 'bible' for MS patients. It shows in detail the results of several decades, tracking hundreds of patients, who followed the Swank low fat diet program. If you commit to reducing your saturated fat intake to 15 grams daily, take a teaspoon of cod liver oil plus a minimum of 3000 milligrams of vitamin C daily, you will feel much better five years from now than you feel today. And if you reduce stress in your life and stay on the program for the rest of your life, MS is unlikely to shorten your life expectancy; it will likely enhance your health as well as your life span."

It is well over thirty years ago when Margaret and I first visited Dr. Swank. We started the low saturated fat, cod liver oil and vitamin C program, and I soon began to feel better. Even after so many years I have no visible evidence of having MS.

In the 1990's I helped Dr. Swank establish the Swank MS Foundation and had the pleasure of working with him for several years.

It is very likely that most of my readers who know someone in their circle of family, friends, or acquaintances, who has MS. It is my hope that this brief synopsis of my experience may give them courage and hope. Most important is, a determination to help themselves, with the proper diet and reducing stress in their life.

I strongly recommend that anyone with MS obtain a copy of Dr. Swank's book; "The Multiple Sclerosis Diet Book" by Roy L. Swank, MD, Ph.D., published by Doubleday, it should be available at most major bookstores or online at Amazon.com.

Sid Baron